Dear Frank,

I am sure this book will bring back a lot of good old memories.

Lots of love,
Joanne + Gerry
Yin Pang + So Yi

May 2000

x x x x

# DARE TO BE WISE

## A HISTORY OF THE MANCHESTER GRAMMAR SCHOOL

# DARE TO BE WISE

## A HISTORY OF THE MANCHESTER GRAMMAR SCHOOL

### JAMES BENTLEY

JAMES X JAMES

IN MEMORY OF FREDERICK RICHARD POSKITT
HEAD OF HISTORY AT MGS, 1926–1933
HEADMASTER OF BOLTON SCHOOL, 1933–1966

## ACKNOWLEDGEMENTS

IN writing this book I was not only given the opportunity to interview the present High Master of the Manchester Grammar School but also his three surviving predecessors, Lord James of Rusholme, Mr Peter Mason and Mr David Maland. In thanking them for giving so much of their time to me, may I also especially thank Mr Peter Laycock, Surmaster of the school, and four other masters, Dr John Cantrell, Mr David Jennings, Mr Nigel Reynolds and, above all, Mr Ian Bailey both for their guidance and for their kindness to an outsider delving into the mysteries of the most famous day school in the world. Finally, working in the local history section of Manchester Central Library gained me a wealth of information and, because of the unstinting helpfulness of its staff, unexpected pleasure.

JAMES BENTLEY,
MAY 1990

The author and publishers are grateful to the following for permission to reproduce pictures:
J. Allan Cash Plate 1 (right); Clifton College p. 81; Hulton Picture Library p. 129 (right); Manchester Central Library pp. 13, 28, 38, 42, 44, 51, 60, 66, 70, 87, 95 and Plate 4; Manchester City Art Galleries Plate 5; Mander and Mitchenson Theatre Collection p. 131 (top); Marks and Spencer PLC pp. 9, 130 (right) and 131 (bottom); Oldham Art Gallery Plate 1 (left); The National Portrait Gallery pp. 129 (left), 130 (centre), 131 (left); Lord Tordoff p. 132 (centre); Solo Syndication p. 125; Universal Pictorial Press and Agency p. 132 (right); by courtesy of the Dean and Chapter of Westminster p. 33.

ISBN 0 907383 041
© The Manchester Grammar School
First published 1990

Typeset by Columns Design and Production Services, Reading
Printed in Great Britain by BAS Printers, Over Wallop, Hampshire
Design by Caroline Archer
Cover design by David Stockwell
Photograph p. 124 by Barney Harford
Other photography by Paul Sweeney
Map p. 133 by Chris Laithwaite

Published by James and James
75 Carleton Road, London N7 0ET

# FOREWORD

Every generation writes history in its own fashion and even if the Manchester Grammar School had not celebrated its 475th anniversary in 1990 there would have been a case for another version of its past to complement, rather than supersede, the works of Mumford (1915) and Graham and Phythian (1965).

There has been a series of happy coincidences. I was very grateful to Sir Roger Young, a distinguished former member of the Common Room, for drawing my attention to the series on famous schools, of which this book is a part. Hamish MacGibbon, the Managing Director of James & James, and I crossed paths at Mons OCS during our National Service, and it has been very pleasant to renew an old friendship and deal, at a more personal level, with the many items of business involved in producing a book of this kind.

In James Bentley we have been most fortunate in finding an author who knew this part of the North well, has worked in another large and famous school, and has a sharp eye for spotting the genius of this particular place. He has been able to combine scholarship with a most agreeable fluency, which makes the reader's passage through some of the less eventful years of the school's early history a pleasant preparation for the more expansive era of the last century or so. He has found new material; inevitably his perception of older matter differs from that of the earlier authors.

Inevitably, too, much of the school's early history is written in terms of its High Masters. In earlier days they often had a lonely responsibility in a much smaller school, but more recently the High Master's most important task has been to assemble and manage a large, powerful and effective team, and it is gratifying that the later chapters give proper recognition to all those members of the Common Room whose ability and dedication have raised the school to its present eminence.

Those High Masters who saw through great changes also had luck. Walker was fortunate to live at the time of Manchester's great expansion. This growth, the city's increased wealth and the development of railways made possible his transformation of the school. Both Paton and Eric James were in office at times of post-war idealism. Then, offering a first-rate academic education to those of promise, regardless of their parents' means, was considered progressive, liberal orthodoxy by governments of all colours. The latter part of this century has, in contrast, seen us on the defensive, anxious to cooperate with, and perhaps complement, the State system, but continually threatened, either by financial penalties or even total closure. Currently, a national system of testing and assessment and a National Curriculum, designed quite understandably for the average child, makes partnership and cooperation with the State system difficult for a selective school like MGS.

Given these uncertainties, some very bold decisions have been taken. Building programmes have become more ambitious; classes are smaller; the range of studies has become more varied; there are more games, more visits, more societies. Indeed, MGS has been described as a model of what a day school of modest means and with a short working day might achieve. Not surprisingly, the school attracts visitors from all over the world. It remains a strong, vibrant institution, forward looking rather than living on its past, though glad for a while to share an interesting past with the readers of this book.

GEOFFREY PARKER
OCTOBER 1989

*Half title page: Hugh Oldham's rebus: owl-dom, his name as he would have pronounced it. The school motto (a quotation from* Horace Epistles *1.2.40) runs below it.*

*Title page: The Manchester Grammar School in the early 1980s, a drawing by Geldart.*

# CONTENTS

## LIST OF COLOUR PLATES

*Plate 1* (facing page 24) Hugh Oldham's tomb; The Oldham Chapelry; Corpus Christi College, Oxford.

*Plate 2* (facing page 25) Humphrey Chetham; Misericords under the High Master's and Usher's seats in Manchester cathedral.

*Plate 3* (facing page 40) Charles Lawson; Owl from the 1776 school; The second Grammar School Building.

*Plate 4* (facing page 41) Lawson's House; Houses in Manchester's Gibraltar area, early nineteenth century.

*Plate 5* (facing page 104) Albert Square, Manchester, 1910.

*Plate 6* (facing page 105) The book of remembrance; The King's colours of the 1st/6th battalion and the 2nd/6th battalion with the regimental colour in Manchester cathedral; The memorial figure; the roll of honour.

*Plate 7* (facing page 120) The main entrance to the 1931 quadrangle; The sports pavilion; The High Master's entrance; The school weather vane.

*Plate 8* (facing page 121) Frederick William Walker; J. L. Paton; Practice at the school's new organ; Detail from carving in front of the organ pipes.

# EPIGRAPH

*'The Manchester Grammar School in every way stands far ahead of any other Secondary School in my district; the advanced character of the education given, the largeness of the area from which it draws its day boys, and the extraordinary number of boys which it sends up annually to the universities, not only distinguish it from other Lancashire schools, but give it a foremost and in some respect the foremost place among the great day schools of England.'*

Report of F. E. Kitchener
to the Royal Commission on
Secondary Education, 1895.

# INTRODUCTION

In the early twentieth century a boy named Simon Marks, the son of a Jewish immigrant from Russian Poland who had set up business with a Yorkshireman named Tom Spencer, entered the Manchester Grammar School. There he shared the same class as the son of a Jewish refugee from Lithuania, a boy called Israel Sieff. Soon the two boys began to do their homework together and they became lifelong friends. One day, as Simon later recorded, he forgot to bring his own homework into school. Mr Horsley, his sixth form master, simply responded that it did not matter. 'He knew how to mark me because he had had Sieff's homework,' wrote Simon.

These two Grammar School boys grew up to marry each other's sisters. Israel Sieff joined the Marks and Spencer Board in 1915 and succeeded Simon Marks as its chairman after his friend's death in 1964. Theirs was a remarkable partnership, and, as we shall see, they remained passionately and generously devoted to their old school.

The presence of two such boys in the school indicates the central connection between the Manchester Grammar School and its seat in a great Northern city.

*Poised for success: the Modern Sixth in 1906, with Israel Sieff second from the right on the back row and his future brother-in-law, Simon Marks, on the far right of the front row.*

9

Both boys were born in a regional capital whose social life flourished, whose Jewish community numbered around twenty-five thousand and whose conurbation included one and a half million people. From this community any boy who could win a place at the school was welcomed.

In 1515 when the school was founded, Manchester and the hundred of Salford by contrast constituted little more than a village. The school, albeit producing notable men from the start and led by High Masters who were sometimes cranks and sometimes geniuses, could also seem remote, like many another provincial grammar school. Indeed the Oxford antiquary Anthony à Wood, writing towards the end of the seventeenth century, was not even sure whether it still existed.

A century and a half later the school's enemies among Manchester radicals almost succeeded in destroying it, managing in 1849 to obtain a decree banning the masters from taking in boarders. Fortunately, the world of Manchester was being transformed. Leaving aside the population of Salford, Manchester itself now comprised some thirty-five thousand homes. And the railway age was dawning. 'Your railroad starts the new era,' W. M. Thackeray perspicaciously observed in 1860. Boarding at a stroke became an anachronism.

For the Manchester Grammar School this new era coincided with the appointment of a superb and visionary High Master, F. W. Walker, whom Benjamin Jowett, Master of Balliol, called 'the finest schoolmaster in England'. As the railways brought him the finest pupils he could attract, Walker set exceedingly high standards, for his masters as well as his boys. They and their successors, many of them equally brilliant men, raised the Manchester Grammar School to a peak of academic, intellectual and cultural excellence from which it has never fallen. The following pages tell the history of this school from its foundation on the eve of the Reformation, by a Lancastrian who had become a Bishop of the Catholic Church, till the present day.

# 1

## An Unassuming Prelude
### 1515–1606

THE founder of what was later to be described as 'the academically most successful school in the world' was, despite his education at both Oxford and Cambridge, by no means a learned man. He was however astute, ambitious, and charitable.

Hugh Oldham, Bishop of Exeter, was born around the year 1460, possibly in Ancoats or perhaps in what was then the village of Oldham, and educated in the household of the Earl of Derby by an Oxford man named Thomas Westbury. The young man went on to study in Oxford as an undergraduate at Exeter College. Then he moved to Cambridge, where he graduated from Queens' College.

Neither then, nor subsequently, was anyone impressed with his brain power. Francis Godwin, writing seventy years after his death, described Hugh as 'A man of more zeale than knowledge, and more devotion than learning; . . . but in deede and action friendly.' Anthony à Wood in his celebrated history of the writers and bishops of Oxford, declared he was but 'partly fitted for Academical Learning,' adding that (unlike most bishops) Hugh Oldham entered his see without the prefix of Dr.

The bishop never bothered even to iron out the cadences of his northern tongue. Hugh Oldham, according to Francis Godwin, was 'somewhat rough in speeche.' Clearly he spoke with a Lancashire (or Oldham) accent, an accent which one observer noted was still giving the boys' conversation a 'porridgy dourness' four and a half centuries later (save when they burst into marvellously mobile French). Anthony à Wood (the seventeenth century historian) offered his readers the phonetical spelling of the bishop's name – Owldham – from which derives the rebus of an owl which formed part of his coat of arms and to this day is the emblem of the school he founded.

In 1485 Hugh Oldham was ordained and became a curate of St Mildred, Bread Street, London. Among his fellow-pupils under Thomas Westbury had been William Smyth, soon to become Bishop of Lincoln, and Hugh profited from the connection by collecting from Smyth the livings of Swinehead,

*Hugh Oldham, D.D. Bishop of Exeter, the founder of the Free Grammar School in Manchester. A nineteenth century engraving by C. Pye from the contemporary portrait in Corpus Christi College, Oxford. The engraving is inscribed to the President of the College.*

Wareboys and Stillingfleet, as well as a canonry of Lincoln cathedral. These were not his only livings. A typically non-resident clergyman of the kind that flourished in the years immediately preceding the Reformation, Oldham followed the common practice of holding several ecclesiastical livings in common (at one time eleven at once).

He prospered and advanced in his profession. In 1503, for instance, he was one of the three men honoured by being invited to lay the foundation stone of Henry VII's chapel in Westminster Abbey. He became chaplain to Margaret, Countess of Richmond. In 1504 he was appointed Archdeacon of Exeter, and in the same year the Bishop of Exeter died. Through the influence of Countess Margaret, Hugh Oldham was consecrated in his place. He was a litigious bishop, and a quarrel with Abbot Bonham of Tavistock became so acrimonious that the abbot finally appealed to the Pope, and Leo X excommunicated Hugh Oldham. The excommunication was lifted only after the bishop's death, enabling him to be buried in the sumptuous tomb he had built for himself in a chapel of his cathedral.

Hugh Oldham was a forward-looking man and an ally of the humanist bishop John Colet. When in 1511 Colet, who had founded St Paul's School in London two years previously, preached on the need for the Reformation of the Church, Oldham had read the epistle at the service. He sensed the swell of opinion against the old religion, the impending changes that were to culminate in the Reformation and the creation of a Protestant establishment in England. Richard Foxe, Bishop of Winchester, asked his advice over setting up a charitable foundation to atone for the sins of his life, and Hugh Oldham urged him not to 'build houses and provide livelihoods for a company of bussing monks, whose end and fall they themselves might live to see'.

'No, no!' he continued, 'it is more meet a great deal that we should have care to provide for the increase of learning, and for such as who by their learning shall do good in the church and commonwealth.' Oldham whose visionary eyes look out from his portrait in Corpus Christi College, Oxford, though not a Protestant Reformer, was thus a man of the renaissance, impatient with some decaying aspects of the old religion and – though no scholar – ready to embrace the New Learning. The college he and Foxe eventually founded at Oxford was the first, either there or at Cambridge, to teach Greek. If the ecclesiastical pluralism which Hugh Oldham himself practised was already coming under attack by the reformers in the church, he had the foresight to use the wealth it helped to bring him to enrich the lives of the poor, in particular the poor of the county in which he was born.

As Francis Godwin rightly insisted, 'Albeit he were not very well learned; yet a great favourer of learning he was.' Hugh Oldham's first plan was to extend both the revenues and the buildings of Exeter College, Oxford. Unfortunately for the college, Godwin tells us, the fellows declined to accept as one of their number a man named Atkins, in spite of the bishop's earnest entreaties on his behalf. They were foolish. Oldham 'altered his determination, and contributed largely towards the formation of Corpus Christi College.' In fact he contributed the huge sum of six thousand marks, 'whereof,' Godwin remarks, 'he is esteemed (and worthily) the principal benefactor.' In consequence the fellows of Corpus were delighted to institute an annual mass, for Oldham's good and happy state during his lifetime, and for his soul after his death. More important from the point of view of the Manchester Grammar School, the seed was sown for a permanent and fruitful link between the college and the school.

'Principal benefactor' of Corpus Christi College, Oxford, Hugh Oldham was without doubt also the chief benefactor of the Manchester Grammar School. In 1516 a clergyman, accountant and chaplain to the bishop named Hugh Bexwyke paid on behalf of Oldham the sum of £5 to buy from George Trafford a piece of land near the River Irk in Manchester. This was the first site of Hugh Oldham's Manchester Grammar School. On 28 April the following year work began on building the school itself. By 10 August 1518 when the school was completed, Hugh Bexwyke had paid to masons and other workmen wages amounting to £12 1s 0d. These wages were lumped in the final account with the cost of lime, sand, stones, timbers, ironwork and other materials, amounting to a final bill of £218 13s 5d.

But even though Lancashire had been educationally and socially backward

*Outside the college gates, Hugh Oldham's original school is the large building on the right: a sketch by local historian T. Barritt.*

13

for centuries, cut off from the prosperity of the rest of the country, education in Manchester did not start with Hugh Oldham's initiative. An embryo of the school he so signally enriched had already been intimately connected with the Collegiate church which is now Manchester Cathedral, and some sort of educational endowment probably dates back as far as the foundation of this Collegiate church in 1420. Almost certainly it reaches to the year 1506, when a Jesus chantry was founded in the Collegiate church.

A chantry, endowed for priests to say mass for the soul of some benefactor, frequently required that such priests also act as schoolmasters. In 1548 when the Protestant reformers dissolved the English chantries, the commissioners ordered to do so came upon such a chantry attached to the Collegiate church in Manchester. It had been founded by a merchant named Alexander Bessike and it supported two priests. Their task was not simply to pray for Bessike's soul but also 'to teach a free school.' This can only be the school described in Hugh Bexwyke's final account as 'the free school of Manchester,' the school Hugh Oldham endowed.

The commissioners of 1548 even named the two priest-schoolmasters of the time: Robert Prestwich and Edward Pendleton. They were paid a little more than £8 a year for their work. These Protestant commissioners decided that the free school should be allowed to continue, with Edward Pendleton in sole charge. They offered him a yearly wage of £4 1s 9d. Their decision was a wise one. As far away as Oxford, Pendleton, the sixth master of Manchester Grammar School since its endownment by Hugh Oldham, was renowned as a teacher. A century and a half later Anthony à Wood described him as 'the famous scholar of Manchester in Lancashire, who, *circa* 1547, was admitted to the reading of any Book in the Faculty of Grammar, that is, to the degree of Bachelor of Grammar.'

The schoolmaster and usher of the Manchester Grammar School already had their own seats in the stalls of the Collegiate church. Today these can be identified by the early sixteenth century carvings, or misericords, which pleasingly illustrated the profession of their incumbents. The chief master (or Archididasculus) sat on the south side between the canons and minor canons. The second master (the usher, under-master or Hypodidasculus) sat opposite on the north side. In the early sixteenth century carving underneath the master's seat the misericord depicts a fox carrying off a headless goose while another fox teaches its cubs to read with a birch over its shoulder. Underneath the usher's seat a female saint – representing knowledge – slays the dragon of ignorance.

Hugh Oldham's objection to 'bussing monks' did not mean that he spurned clergymen either as schoolmasters or as trustees of his foundations. For nearly a hundred years other schools had been founded with the specific injunctions that their trustees should be laymen and their masters not clerics. But when Hugh Oldham came to endow his grammar school in Manchester he set such sentiments to one side. According to the deeds of 1515 only one layman was to serve as a trustee; the other trustees were drawn from the warden and fellows of the Collegiate church in Manchester – all of them priests – and one of the

*Manchester's Collegiate Church, whose educational endowment was the embryo for Hugh Oldham's school. Engraved in 1832 by J. Le Keux from a drawing by N. G. Philips.*

most important trustees was the Abbot of Whalley. If the warden and fellows of the Collegiate church failed to appoint a master and usher, the abbot was empowered to do so.

As for the schoolmasters themselves, the foundation deed of 1515 declared that they could be either monks or secular clergymen. They could be removed only 'for reasonable cause, such as incontinence, or neglect of their scholars.'

Oldham's generosity went far beyond the cash he paid through Hugh Bexwyke for buying the site and building the school. In addition he endowed the school with lands by the River Irk, and the profits of water-driven corn mills. The lord of the manor (which now became the school) could legally oblige every tenant or resident of the manor to grind their corn and malt here, paying fees to the school for doing so. A 'walk' mill (so-called because water was mixed with fuller's earth, the cloth was laid in it and then walked on) provided further income.

The whole purpose, as the deed of endowment stated, was to provide a schoolmaster, 'eminent for wisdom, character and virtue,' to ensure that 'grace, virtue and wisdom should grow, flower, and take root in youths during their boyhood, especially in boys of the county of Lancaster, who for a long time through the default of teaching and instruction had lacked such grace, virtue and wisdom in their youth, both through their father's poverty and through the absence and want of such a teacher.'

William Plessyngton, paid £10 a year (in four instalments) was appointed first master; Richard Wulstoncroft was made first usher, paid £5, likewise in quarterly instalments. They were given twenty days holiday a year to 'sport' themselves. The sums of £10 and £5 were to be their whole wage, for they had to swear to teach all their boys and scholars equally well, taking no presents or gifts from any of them.

Their job, Oldham specified, was to teach grammar in Manchester just as it was then taught 'in the school of the town of Banbury in the county of Oxford now there taught, which is called Stanbridge grammar'. In prescribing John Stanbridge's grammar for use in his new school the bishop was acknowledging the remarkable reputation of the works of a man who had been master of Magdalen College School, Oxford till his death in 1510. Stanbridge was, said Anthony à Wood, 'naturally delighted in the faculty of Grammar' and became so happy in his profession (which, Wood added, 'is esteemed by the generality a drudgery') that when he reached old age instead of retiring and living off what he had saved from earlier years he cheerfully continued teaching, living 'poor and bare to his last, yet with a juvenile and cheerful spirit'.

Hugh Oldham's prescription enables us to see how the very first Manchester masters taught Latin at his Grammar School. Stanbridge taught children to say 'Good morrow' and 'Good night' to each other in Latin. Boys would learn translations of edifying remarks, such as 'Scholars must live hardily at Oxford,' and 'Wysshers and wolders be small householders,' as well as how to say in Latin such doleful news as 'My father had a great loss on the sea.'

Generations would have opened their grammars to be confronted by Stanbridge's opening sentences: 'What is to be done when an English is given to be made into Latin? First the verb must be looked out, and if there be more verbs than one in a reason, I must look out the principle verb and ask the question who or what, and that word that answers to the question shall be the nominative case to the verb. Except it be a verb Impersonal, the which will have no nominative case.'

At very many grammar and public schools, Stanbridge's methods of teaching Latin prevailed for a remarkably long time, taught in variously amended editions of his works until superseded by Kennedy's Latin primer only in 1870. Manchester (and Merchant Taylors') were exceptional in abandoning the drudgery of Stanbridge in 1660 and substituting a more amenable *Delectus of Latin Phrases* by Thomas Bracebridge.

As well as teaching, the master and usher were also obliged to put on surplices and attend service in the choir of the Collegiate church on feast days; and on 4 March they were required solemnly to pray for the souls of Hugh Oldham himself, his parents Roger and Mary, and his brother Bernhard, who was Archdeacon of Cornwall.

On 25 June 1519 Hugh Oldham died. Six years later the school was given a new charter. In the meantime one of Oldham's solicitors, John Hulme, appointed to make sure that the master and usher were paid, tried instead to take the profit from the mills and the land by the River Irk for his own personal use. The second charter constituted an entirely new form of government for the school. From now on twelve lay trustees (known as feoffees) were to administer the revenues of the school. Whenever their number dwindled to four, they were to be replenished by the election of 'honest gentlemen and honest persons' who lived in the parish of Manchester. The High Master was now to be appointed by Hugh and Joan Bexwyke, and after the death of one or both of them, by the president of the Oxford College, Corpus Christi, founded by Richard Foxe with Oldham's aid. The warden of the Collegiate church could still dismiss him. As for the Abbot of Whalley, his powers were now reduced to appointing the school treasurer (or receiver, as he was and still is called) and holding, along with three other persons, one of the keys to the school's treasure chest.

The principal aim, as the preamble to the deed declared, was 'the bringing up in learning, virtue and good manners' of the children of Lancashire, long suffering 'for lack of sufficient Schoolmaster and usher there, so that the children in the same country having pregnant wits have been for the most part brought up rudely and idley and not in virtue, cunning, erudition, literature, and in good manners.' The aim was 'for a Free School there to be kept for evermore and to be called Manchester School'.

Whether the master was a priest or a layman was still considered unimportant, provided that he was 'honest of his living and whole of body, as not being vexed or infected with any continual infirmity or dissease, and having sufficient litterature and learning to be a Schoolmaster, and able to teach children grammar.' And the deed of 1525 was more radical than Hugh Oldham's foundation charter in one other respect: now the president of Corpus was expressly forbidden to appoint a monk as High Master.

The first school admitted not just boys from Lancashire. Quite specifically no male child was to be excluded from any part of the country, provided he suffered from no contagious disease or infection, such as 'pox, leprosy, pestilence'. Each scholar, on admission to the school, was to donate a penny, to be given to two poor scholars appointed by the High Master or usher who would clean the building. No child was allowed to bring any weapon, such as a dagger or a stave, into the school (save for a meat knife). No boy was to eat food in the school, but those coming a great distance could bring food and eat it in some house in the town. School started at six in the morning (seven in winter). Cock-fighting and jousting were severely frowned on. The senior boys, instead of wasting time and money on such unlawful pursuits, were expected to help the master and usher in teaching their younger fellows the alphabet and the rudiments of grammar.

The regime was religious as well as educational. The day began with the High Master or usher leading the scholars in reciting Psalm 67: 'God be merciful unto us and bless us,' though of course in Latin. It ended with the recital of the *Magnificat* and a *De Profundis* for the soul of Hugh Oldham, of his father and mother, and other former benefactors of the school.

Almost immediately the Reformation brought changes. Prayers for the dead

17

were regarded as heretical by the Protestant reformers. In October 1536 a Yorkshireman named Robert Aske, fellow of Gray's Inn, led between thirty thousand and forty thousand men in a 'pilgrimage of grace' protesting against the suppression of the English monasteries. Even King Henry VIII received him with favour, promising to redress the grievances; but when disorders broke out again the promises were forgotten and in 1537 Aske was hanged. John Paslow, the twenty-fifth Abbot of Whalley, had joined the pilgrimage, and the Earl of Shrewsbury hanged him at Lancaster. That was the end of the school's connection with Whalley Abbey.

Two famous sons of the school took different sides in the subsequent religious conflicts. John Bradford, the Protestant martyr had been born in the Blackley district of Manchester in 1510 and was educated at the Grammar School. He became a trusted servant of Sir John Harrington, treasurer of the king's camps and buildings, and was deputy paymaster at the siege of Montreuil. Bradford helped his master to swindle the crown out of a considerable amount of money, before beginning to study common law at the Inner Temple. There his friendship with Thomas Sampson, a future Dean of Christ Church, Oxford, turned Bradford's thoughts to studying religion. He heard Hugh Latimer, himself to be burned at the stake, preach on corruption, and repenting of his former greed sold his own jewels to give to the poor. Bradford even gave back the money he and Harrington had cheated from the crown. Although Bradford later admitted he was shielding his former master, at this time he claimed to be solely responsible for the offence.

*John Bradford, an Old Mancunian born in 1510 in Blackley, Manchester and burnt as a protestant martyr, at the stake at Smithfield in 1555.*

Christianity now deeply moved this Manchester Protestant. His friend Sampson recorded how for long periods he would sit utterly silent among his companions, and as he meditated on Jesus 'plenty of tears would trickle down his cheeks.' Bradford was ordained, and his talents speedily brought him the admiration and friendship of several leading protestants, including Martin Bucer and the redoubtable John Knox. Eventually he was appointed chaplain to Nicholas Ridley, Bishop of London. Soon he was one of Edward VI's chaplains in ordinary, licensed to preach anywhere and making a powerful impression proclaiming the Reformed faith throughout the country. From the pulpit he would habitually condemn 'whoredom, adultery, uncleanness, wantonness, idolatry, witchcraft, ennvie, strife, contention, wrath, sedition, murders, drunkenness, gluttony. blasphemy, slothfulness, idleness, bawdy talking, slaunderings'. He described these sins as the 'birds of the devil,' ready to 'broach and eat you.' Thus, as Foxe's *Book of Martyrs* put it, 'he persuaded to the godly life'.

The death of the Protestant Edward VI and the accession of Mary Tudor made his martyrdom inevitable. Bradford himself, lamenting the king's passing, exclaimed 'Our sins made holy Edward die,' a phrase which passed into Puritan lore and was reused (and acknowledged as Bradford's) by preachers a century later on the death of Oliver Cromwell. The outcome of Bradford's trial for heresy was foreordained. Condemned, he was at first to be burned in Manchester, but many feared that the people would rise up to protect him. Instead, on 30 June 1555 he was taken to Smithfield along with another Protestant martyr named John Leaf. The fires were lit at nine o'clock the following morning. Bradford first took up a faggot and kissed it. Then, with the sheriff's consent he undressed and gave his clothing to his servant. He began to declaim against false religion, but the sheriff threatened to tie his hands if he would not be quiet. Bradford replied, 'O master sheriff, I am quiet. God forgive you this, master sheriff.' Then he said to John Leaf, 'Be of good comfort, brother, for we shall have a merry supper this night.' As he died, he repeated the words, 'Strait is the way and narrow is the gate that leadeth to salvation, and few there be that find it.'

Touchingly, as he languished in gaol awaiting martyrdom, John Bradford's mind turned back to his days at the Manchester Grammar School. The prisoner wrote his *Godly Meditations upon the Lords Prayer, the Beleefe, and ten Commandments,* to be published after his death. When he came to the fifth commandment, 'Honour thy father and thy mother,' Bradford felt constrained to thank God not simply for them alone but also his tutors and masters. 'I cannot but say that I have most cause to thank thee for my Parents, Schoolmasters and others under whose tuition thou has put me,' he declared, adding, 'no pen is able to write the particular benefits which I have hereby received in my infancy, childhood, youth, middle age, and always hitherto.' His parents and teachers seemed to him to have represented the goodness of God himself. 'O how good a Lord hast thou declared thyself to me, within them,' Bradford exclaimed, 'and by them hast nourished, fed, instructed, corrected, defended and most graciously kept me. I could reckon innumerable behind me, and but few before me, so much made of and cared for as I have been hitherto.'

So he ended with a prayer that all in positions of authority might display the virtues of his home and his Grammar School. 'Give unto the hearts of all Parents, Masters and such as be in authority here or elsewhere, that they may according to that thou hast put in them in trust withall, be faithful, diligent, careful, and happy.'

Another boy of the Manchester Grammar School, Laurence Vaux, a devout and creative Catholic of the same troubled era, though he managed to escape martyrdom, is the mirror image of John Bradford. Born at Blackrod some ten years later than Bradford, after studying at the school he went first to Queen's College, Oxford, and then to Foxe's new foundation, Corpus Christi College. The Bishop of Chester ordained him priest in 1542, and he became a fellow of the Collegiate church next to his old school just in time for the college to be dissolved by the Protestants in the first year of the reign of Edward VI.

Vaux survived as a curate in Manchester until the accession of Mary Tudor led to the refounding of the Collegiate church. He became a fellow again and eventually warden. Evidently a gentle man, when the Catholics used his college partly to imprison Protestants, Vaux by their own account treated them with kindness. He was also a man of foresight. With the accession of the Protestant Elizabeth I Vaux refused to take the oath of supremacy which recognised her as supreme governor of the Church in England. Taking with him the Collegiate church plate, its vestments and its muniments, he fled to Ireland. Soon Vaux was in Louvain, teaching the children of Catholic exiles. In 1566 he was in Rome, where Pope Pius V instructed him that on no account were English Catholics to attend divine service in the Anglican church. It was a message Vaux conveyed home, but he had managed to return safely from England back to Louvain by 1567. Although some Irish thieves had robbed

*The choir at the Collegiate Church, Manchester, where boys prayed daily for their pious founder's soul until the reformation. A nineteenth century engraving from a drawing by I. Palmer.*

him of part of Manchester's church plate, Vaux drew up documents providing for the return of the rest to their rightful home on the day the Collegiate church should return to the Catholic faith.

He was busy writing a Catholic *Cathechism of Christian Doctrine, necessary for Children and Ignorant People* and helping to set up the Catholic college at Douai in France. His cathechism published, Vaux joined the Jesuits Parsons and Campion in attempting to reconvert his own country. At Rochester in 1580 he was captured by the Protestants, and the Bishop of London imprisoned him in the gatehouse at Westminster. Remarkably Vaux escaped martyrdom, and indeed lived for a time, as he put it, 'well content with my state,' paying £16 a year for his room, joined by many friends in worship. Imprisonment grew more rigorous after he had been transferred from Westminster gatehouse to the Clink in Southwark; but sectarian passions were less strong than in the reign of Mary Tudor, his Protestant captors inclined to spare his life, and he died peacefully in 1585. Naturally enough, back in Louvain his fellow-Catholics insisted that martyr's chains had killed him.

Meanwhile, what of the High Master of the Manchester Grammar School during these dangerous, dogma-torn times? The Revd Edward Pendleton, son of a Manchester merchant and probably an alumnus of the school, had been educated at Oxford and became High Master in 1547 or thereabouts during the extremely Protestant regime under Edward VI. He survived the Counter-Reformation in England, successfully adapting his conscience to the Catholicism of Mary Tudor (even attempting to controvert the missionary zeal of John Bradford), and then to the Anglicanism of Elizabeth I. Edward Pendleton thus earned from one of the historians of the school the rebuke that 'He is one of the three whose claim to the dignity of being the original hero of the *Vicar of Bray* is an unsettled literary problem.'

Pendleton taught a future Master of Queens' College, Cambridge, William Chadderton, a Puritan reformer who after leaving Cambridge became warden of the Collegiate church in Manchester and then Bishop of Chester. Here Chadderton endeavoured to counteract the religious undercurrents in Lancashire which had nurtured Laurence Vaux. Appointed an ecclesiastical commissioner for the north of England in 1580, he transferred his residence to Manchester and set about fining and imprisoning recusant Catholic families. Their children were then sent to good protestant schools – sometimes to little avail, for between Chadderton's appointment as a commissioner and the end of Elizabeth's reign, of the twenty-two Lancastrians who proceeded to Oxford or Cambridge at least nine decided to cross the channel to Catholic Douai.

Little is known of Pendleton's three successors as High Master, William Terrill, James Bateson and Richard Rayton. Bateson was evidently a scholar, a graduate of Brasenose College in Oxford. One of his pupils, Henry Bury, was to found Bury Grammar School. In 1583 with the appointment of Thomas Cogan as High Master, an unusual scholar and entertaining character brought his influence onto the school.

Born at Chard in Somerset, Cogan was a physician and a teacher, a graduate of Oxford in medicine as well as the classics. In 1574 his own college, Oriel, made him a fellow, a post he resigned on coming to Manchester. A devout man, he had already written *The Well of Wisdome, conteining chief and chosen sayinges gathered out of the Five Bookes of the olde Testament, 1577.* Arriving in Manchester he made a judicious marrige with a rich widow, Ellen Willet, one of the sisters of Sir Edmund Trafford.

As well as teaching, Cogan continued to practise as a doctor of medicine. His curious and lively mind made little distinction between the two professions, for he strongly believed that a healthy body promoted a healthy mind. A year after coming to Manchester he published *The Haven of Health* a book which, as its subtitle declared, had been, 'Chiefly gathered for the comfort of students, and consequently for all those that have a care of their health.' Its epigraph (Ecclesiasticus chapter 37, verse 30) neatly encapsulated the amalgam of devout Christian, pedagogue, and physician which Cogan was: 'By surfeit have many perished; but he that dieteth himself prolongeth his life.'

His principal aim was to prove 'that meates and drinkes doe alter our bodies.' As he pointed out, 'whoso hath commonly an aking head,' he asked, 'if it proceede from a hote cause, shall feele that by drinking strong drinke, the pain will be increased.' Again, argued Cogan, 'whoso hath a wound or sore to be healed, shal find that by eating fresh Beefe, Goose and Garlick, Pigeons and Eelles, and such like, the cure will not come so fast forward as otherwise it would.' He continued 'Wherefore I say to the Gentleman that hath the Gowt (for poore men seldome have it, because for the most parte it groweth thorow excesse and ease) I say that although the forbearing of wine and women, and other things noysome in that disease, doe not utterly take away the gowt, yet it will abate, qualifie and abridge the paine, and make it more tolerable.'

Before going on to discuss in enormous detail the various effects of meat, vegetable, drink and various remedies, Cogan devoted two chapters to the life of the student, chapters richly informative of what life must have been like under this delightful man at the Grammar School.

Chapter 1 of his book, 'What Labor is', lauds the benefit of exercise. The physician speaks in the maxim, 'The colour of the urine showeth when we should exercise' and again in praising the 'Faire property of holsome ayer.' The schoolmaster (or rather, gymnastics master) appears in the judgement that 'Tennise play is the best exercise of all other.' Cogan deplored 'dice, tables, and cardes and such like'. Chess, however, he commended as 'an earnest exercise of the minde, and very commendable and convenient for studentes'.

'Of studie or exercise of the minde in what order we may studie without hindrance of our health,' which is chapter 2 of *The Haven of Health*, offers yet more insights into what the school must have been like overseen by Cogan. Holding that 'Idlenesse is against nature,' he deplored what he described as slothful scholars lying in bed. 'The best time for studies is in the morning,' he held, adding that studies should begin with prayer. Then a student ought to read and meditate on his reading for an hour or so. A brief rest should follow, occupied with combing back one's hair for about forty times with an ivory comb and rubbing one's teeth with a coarse linen cloth. Two more hours of study, interspersed with small intermissions, would take the students to noon, when they would eat according to the wholesome advice of the rest of the book.

Students might work after lunch for perhaps another two hours, provided the day was not too hot, but Cogan felt that the afternoons and the evenings were far less profitable for study than the mornings. Even so, as he observed, it was 'Better to be pale with studie than love.'

He loved and recommended music for reviving the mind wearied with study, 'not only for solace and recreation but also because it moveth man to virtue and good manners and prevaileth greatly to wisdom, quietness of mind and contemplation.' Here, however, this excellent schoolmaster perceived that his pupils needed to develop their own powers of choice, for he insisted, 'But what kind of music every student should use I refer to their own inclination.'

Thomas Cogan resigned as High Master in 1597. Two years earlier he had given some beautifully bound medical works to his old Oxford College, and a note in Latin in the college register, records that the master and fellows unanimously agreed to remit and forgive a debt of 40s which he owed them. They also presented him with a pair of gloves.

He continued to live in Manchester, where he died in 1607, to be buried in the Collegiate church on 10 June. He left behind, as Anthony à Wood observed, 'the character of an able Physician and Latinist, a good Neighbour, and an honest Man'.

His will bequeathed books to the Collegiate church and to the town's apothecaries, and also 4d for every scholar of his school. Such munificence towards the pupils was not new. The second foundation deed of 1525 had decreed that whenever there was more than £40 in the school chest the surplus should provide exhibitions for the old boys who were then studying at Oxford and Cambridge. No scholar was to have more than 26s 8d a year, and the exhibition was to cease when a scholar became fellow of a college or else was granted another exhibition amounting to 7 marks.

Later in the century John Smith, president of Magdalene College, Cambridge and a former pupil of the School, founded scholarships for the those following his footsteps from Manchester to university. William Birch, an old boy, became warden of the Collegiate church and in 1575 bequeathed 40s each to twenty poor scholars of his old school.

The philanthropy of many such men extended beyond the school itself, a generosity displayed supremely by one of Cogan's pupils, Humphrey Chetham. His profession was merchant and manufacturer of woollen cloth. Soon he was rich, and used part of his wealth to help his needy fellows. As high sheriff of Lancashire he helped to raise cash to rebuild St Paul's Cathedral. Towards the end of his life Humphrey Chetham adopted twenty-two poor boys from Manchester, Salford and Droylsden, and in 1648 conceived the idea of setting up a college for them in Manchester. Three years later he was dead, his scheme still unaccomplished, but his will bequeathed

*Humphrey Chetham, Old Mancunian and philanthropist whose executors bought the fifteenth century building abutting the Grammar School in 1651 to house Chetham's Hospital, his foundation for maintaining and educating forty, poor, Lancashire boys.*

£7,000 to found and endow a 'hospital' for maintaining and educating forty poor Lancashire boys. Another legacy was £1,100 plus the residue of his property to set up a public library in Manchester. And he left money to install 'Godly Public Libraries' in several Lancashire churches.

His executors seized the opportunity to buy a fine fifteenth century building close by the Grammar School, and by 1651 this had become the famous Chetham's Hospital, a worthy monument to a man whose elder brother Edward had succeeded Thomas Cogan as High Master of the Manchester Grammar School, and who himself was one of Cogan's brightest pupils.

Nearly a century of religious strife had been successively weathered by Hugh Oldham's school, with such pupils as Bradford and Vaux displaying more commitment than the trimming High Master Edward Pendleton. After the long reign of Elizabeth I the Grammar School could hope to look forward to a more peaceful future. In fact the next hundred years saw its fortunes ebb and flow alarmingly.

*Humphrey Chetham's hospital.*

PLATE 1

*Top: Hugh Oldham's resplendent tomb in Exeter cathedral. 'He lyeth in a church of his own building, cast out of the uppermost ende of the South wall of the Church, where he hath a sumptuous and faire monument.' (Francis Godwin,* A Catalogue of the Bishops of England, *1601) Old Mancunian Keith Mercer surveys the tomb.*

*Left: The Oldham chapelry and surrounding buildings, an eighteenth century painting by James Carse. In the lower right hand corner is the cottage where some say Hugh Oldham was born.*

*Right: Corpus Christi College, Oxford, endowed by Hugh Oldham. The President of Corpus appointed the High Master and Usher for 350 years, and is still an ex-officio governor of the school.*

PLATE 2

*Top: Humphrey Chetham's memorial in Manchester cathedral. An old boy of the Grammar School, he was a merchant philanthropist who founded Chetham's Hospital for poor boys in 1651.*

*Left: The misericord under the High Master's seat in the choir in the Cathedral. The carving on the left shows a fox teaching its cubs to read, with a birch over its shoulder.*

*Right: Under the Usher's seat a female saint (representing knowledge) issuing from a whelk shell slays the dragon of ignorance.*

# 2

## High Notes, Low Notes

### 1606–1764

IF the Manchester Grammar School triumphantly survived the turbulent sixteenth century, its fortunes in the following 200 years were less than brilliant. Scholarly and industrious High Masters were followed by others who totally neglected their duties; some were dismissed and indulged in lengthy recriminations with the feoffees; while a fourth group of masters slumbered happily without contributing greatly to the esteem of the school or the welfare of its pupils.

In any case the seventeenth century began unpropitiously in Manchester with a plague of 1605 that killed around 20,000 people, including a master named George Stursaker. The following year Edward Chetham died, and John Reynolds, the Puritan president of Corpus Christi College, Oxford, appointed Thomas Clayton as his successor. Clayton remained High Master for a decade, making little mark on the school and doing it no harm.

His successor, John Rowland, a fellow of Corpus, was less diligent. Instead of running the school Rowland preferred to serve as chaplain to Henry Montague, first Earl of Manchester, leaving the boys in the care of his brother. From the start Rowland was a disgruntled High Master, for he left Corpus believing that his annual salary would be worth £100 per annum and on arrival in Manchester discovered he was to be paid but £20. In addition, he claimed, at the time of his resignation as an Oxford don he was close to becoming a Doctor of Divinity. To live on an annual salary of £20 holding a position which, he claimed, 'cost me almost as much money out of my own purse' was, he said, a disgrace.

Rowland claimed the approval of some of the feoffees in his decision to abandon his pupils to his brother. If so, the other feoffees disagreed and disapproved of the substitute High Master. Rowland was dismissed. He wrote a spirited letter of protest to the feoffees. Not only had some feoffees approved of his brother, 'both for his life and learning,' he protested, 'and so had the town.' As for his own behaviour, John Rowland claimed that he had 'committed noe offence, worthy of expulsion, only with your leave I have endeavoured to promote myself.'

He also alleged that part of the problem lay with Sir Cecil Trafford, who had at first agreed with his plans but then taken a dislike to his brother. Rowland's letter now tried three tacks.

First conciliation: he promised that 'If my brother have justly offended Sir Cecil or any of the Feoffees, he shall confess his fault and amend.' Next ingratiation: he declared that the Earl of Manchester, was well disposed to the town, had recently sent the citizens a brace of bucks, and with Rowland's encouragement would prove yet more generous in the future. Third the threat of litigation: Rowland rightly pointing out that 'I know well the founder gave the feoffees noe power either to put the High Master out or in.'

This was Rowland's best argument. According to the foundation deeds the one person able to dismiss a High Master was the warden of the Collegiate church, and at that time the Collegiate church had been temporarily dissolved. As the High Master threatened the feoffees, 'I pray be not offended if I make triall to recover my School by law if I cannot regain it by Love.' Although the record is not clear, and some historians declare that Rowland was dismissed in 1630, he probably recovered his position as High Master. At any rate he did not take a benefice until 1634, retiring to Foots Cray in Kent.

Such quarrels cannot have enhanced the educational role of the school. Nor did the man who succeeded Rowland, a Lancastrian from Prestwich named Thomas Harrison. Though a student at Corpus Christi, Harrison matriculated at All Souls College in 1625. Three years later he took his BA degree at Corpus. Harrison was in his late twenties when appointed High Master. He lasted scarcely five years, leaving to become rector of Crick in Northampton-shire and a canon of Lichfield. In 1645 he and his family were ejected from the canonry, his house was burgled, his books were stolen and he was thrown in gaol as a debtor. Francis Mosley, one of his friends from his days as High Master, took pity and in 1661 made a collection for him, to little avail. Harrison remained in gaol.

A Cambridge man succeeded Harrison. Robert Symonds had been head master at Nantwich school since 1634 and might have brought new order into the affairs of the Manchester Grammar School. Unfortunately he stayed barely a year, giving way in 1638 to a notable careerist named Ralph Brideoak.

Born at Cheetham Hill, Manchester, Brideoak had been educated first at the Grammar School and then at Brasenose College, Oxford. There he relished the merriment caused by performances of Ben Jonson's plays, and when Jonson died Brideoak wrote one of the odes in his memory that were published with Jonson's works. He was also a diligent scholar and in 1636 became chaplain of New College. His career was promising. Soon he was a curator of the University Press and a friend of Dr John Jackson, Vice-Chancellor of the university and President of Corpus, who appointed him High Master of his old school. Brideoak brought the school to participate fully in the stirring and dangerous events which were leading to the Civil War.

When the parliamentarians stepped up their attack on the Stuarts in 1640, Brideoak's pupils gave public readings of Latin poems congratulating the Queen on the birth of her son. Brideoak induced them to write speeches commemorating the victory of the English over the Scots, which never happened. Disliking the Puritans, he became chaplain and secretary to the Royalist Earl of Derby, who was soon to be executed in nearby Bolton. Brideoak continued to manage the Earl's estates, and with considerable bravery made his way to London when Derby was taken at the battle of Worcester to plead in vain for his life. It was a generous and apparently foolhardy act that was to pay dividends.

Inevitably, with the execution of Charles I and the exile of his son, Brideoak lost his living. With considerable adroitness he became a turncoat and chaplain to Speaker Lenthall, who had been much impressed by Brideoak's pleas on behalf of the Earl of Derby. In spite of some Cromwellian anger that Lenthall was protecting a man known to be a 'malignant', the Speaker managed to obtain for Brideoak the livings of Witney in Oxfordshire and Long Molton in Norfolk, as well as making him Master of the Rolls. As Speaker Lenthall lay dying it was to the former Royalist High Master of the Manchester Grammar School that he turned for comfort.

Yet Brideoak lived long enough to have his reward for being so long a Royalist. The Queen's son, whom he and his pupils had acclaimed in 1640, became King Charles II. The returning monarch made him rector of St Bartholomew's in London and one of his chaplains. Brideoak became in turn a canon of Windsor (combining this with the rich living of Standish in Lancashire) and Dean of Salisbury, finally bribing Charles II's mistress, the Duchess of Portsmouth, to procure for him the bishopric of Chichester. He combined the revenues of Chichester with those of Standish and Windsor. And he was also made a feoffee of his old school.

At the age of 64 he died, and his widow Mary placed in the chapel of St George's, Windsor, a monument inscribed (in Latin):

Ripe for God
The Reverend Father in Christ RALPH BRIDEOAK
put off mortality.

He was, the inscription continued, 'a man bravely upright, great but humble, and a mighty storehouse of all Attic and eloquence.' He was, his wife's eulogy insisted, 'kind to strangers, a lover of good men, and a father, so to speak, of his diocese.'

Whether this man who, as Anthony à Wood commented, 'had spent the chief part of his life in continual agitation, for the obtaining of Wealth and setling a Family (for he was a married Man and left behind him three Sons at his death)' might be considered a fit example for the children of the owl is debatable. One of his more questionable acts was to obtain £200 compensation for some market stalls burned down outside St Bartholomew's during the

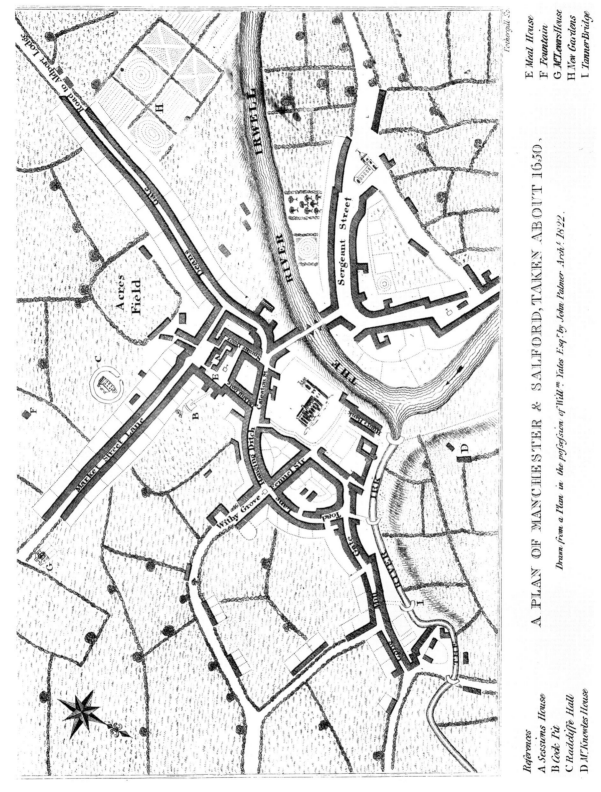

A PLAN OF MANCHESTER & SALFORD, TAKEN ABOUT 1650.

Drawn from a Plan in the possession of Will.ᵐ Yates Esq.ʳ by John Palmer Arch.ᵗ 1822.

References
A Sessions House
B Cock Pit
C Radcliffe Hall
D Mᶜ Knowles House

E Meal House
F Fountain
G Mᶜ Lewers House
H New Gardens
I Tanner-Bridge

great fire of London in 1666, and then keep the money for himself. Yet in enormously perilous times he impressed many wise men of widely different persuasions, and he survived.

Meanwhile the school had been in some disarray. A Cambridge man named Nehemiah Painter, Brideoak's successor as High Master, had been appointed in 1645 and died three years later. That he kept the standard of the school as high as it was under Brideoak was a remarkable achievement, for the defeat of Charles I in the civil war meant that Painter and the Royalist feoffees fled the city and the school was closed.

On 6 March 1647 the citizens of Manchester petitioned the Government to appoint new feoffees. Only six of the previous ones survived. Sir Alexander Radcliffe, knighted at Charles I's coronation, had raised troops for the king and had allied with the Earl of Derby during the siege of Lathom House; Baron Rochdale had fought on the King's side both at Edgehill and at Worcester; and Sir Cecil Trafford was not only a noted Royalist whose men had fought for the King at Shrewsbury but in 1632 had also converted to Roman Catholicism, the religion of Charles I's hated Queen Henrietta Maria. Two others, Robert Holland and Richard Radcliffe were more acceptable to the Presbyterians who now ruled the land, for the former belonged to a family long noted for its Puritanism and the latter was himself a Presbyterian and had fought on the parliamentary side during the civil war. The final surviving feoffee was Robert Hyde of Denton, of whose views we are ignorant.

Surprisingly enough, as well as confirming Robert Hyde, Robert Holland and Richard Radcliffe as feoffees, parliament also retained Sir Alexander Radcliffe. Eight other distinguished local men, all of them loyal to the parliamentary cause, brought the number of feoffees up to full strength. The Court of Sequestrators then directed that the feoffees transfer the lease of the school mills from the Royalist Edmund Prestwich to the parliamentarian John Hartley.

Almost immediately these new feoffees, ignoring the President of Corpus Christi College, Oxford, were faced with appointing a new High Master. They chose another turncoat, though this time a man (unlike Ralph Brideoak) whose conversion to the cause of Parliament from that of the King was genuine.

John Wickens had been made head master of Rochdale School in 1638 by Archbishop Laud, who had been executed for supporting Charles I. At the same time as appointing Wickens, Laud made his own nephew, Robert Bath, vicar of Rochdale. Wickens and Bath not only struck up a friendship, but both men converted to Presbyterianism and became leading elders in the Bury Classis, the ruling body of the local Presbyterian church. Wickens married Penelope Chadwick, daughter of a distinguished Puritan who was rector of Standish.

This was the man made High Master of the Manchester Grammar School in succession to Nehemiah Painter (with whose family he clearly remained in close contact, for one of Wickens' daughters married Painter's son, Stephen).

*Opposite: Rural Manchester and Salford, a plan drawn in about 1650 with Long Millgate flanking the River Irk and the School and Chetham's Hospital between them. Note the unconventional orientation.*

29

The new High Master proved an excellent choice. A cultured, scholarly man and a fine teacher, Wickens also attracted to the school the sons of many of the leading Puritan families in the county and beyond. He established warm relations with Chetham's librarian, who gave permission for Wickens' best pupils to use the library in return for acting as part-time librarians.

In consequence the educational standards established by Brideoak at the Grammar School and continued by Painter were enhanced, and in spite of the upheavals of the two decades between 1640 and 1660, eleven Manchester scholars went from the school to Oxford and fifty-five to Cambridge – far more than at any other comparable period in the century – for the most part to train for the Christian ministry.

The restoration of the Stuarts caused considerable consternation to the school, even though many Presbyterians now welcomed their return. On 22 April 1661 a noted Royalist, Sir Nicholas Mosley, led the celebrations in Manchester for the coronation of Charles II. Colours flying and drums beating, Mosley's company paraded through the streets ahead of forty uniformed young boys carrying miniature weapons, who were followed by some older boys carrying muskets and pikes. Then everyone laid down his arms and entered the Collegiate church for an act of worship. After the service the procession re-formed, accompanied by the boroughreeve, the burgesses, the constables and Sir Ralph Assheton, who, though his father had been a parliamentary general, had become a staunch Royalist.

Sir Cecil Trafford, ejected from the body of the feoffees in 1647, was determined to force his way back. In 1660 the new principal Secretary of State, Sir Edward Nicholas, had already appointed or reappointed twelve men drawn from both sides in the previous conflicts and including Ralph Assheton. When Ralph Holland died Trafford managed to replace him and also persuaded parliament to replace five of the other feoffees with his own men – one of them Ralph Brideoak. They now proceeded to eject John Hartley as licensee of the school mills and replace him by Sir Nicholas Mosley.

Momentarily John Wickens' own position was in danger. He had been appointed illegally, without reference to the president of Corpus; and he was a known presbyterian. Happily, the new feoffees chosen in 1660 included one of his old pupils, a lawyer named William Butterworth, who had survived Trafford's coup. Wickens had been his only schoolmaster, and Butterworth gratefully confessed that this was the man 'to whom I owe what I am'.

As a member of Gray's Inn Butterworth had also been helped by a relative named John Nicholas, now one of the Secretaries of State, whom Wickens was urgently soliciting. In September 1660 the former pupil wrote to Nicholas, thanking the Secretary of State for the 'many favours I received from you and the great candor I found in you, during my short stay in London'. These had emboldened him to write on behalf of 'this my worthy friend', John Wickens.

'The School at Manchester (for which he comes to solicit) being of an Episcopal and brave foundation, is likely now to be ruined, except upholden by the Secretaries, and your gracious assistance,' Butterworth wrote. 'I doubt not but that your owne love of learning will be a great motive to your speedy and effectual dispatch hereof; which I am the more urgent to move you to do, by reason of the honour that will accrue to you thereby, when it shall be known that by your means alone this ancient foundation is revived from its ashes and restored to its pristine splendour.' William Butterworth's intercession was successful, and John Wickens was confirmed as High Master of the Grammar School.

He did not desert his former nonconformist friends, and indeed used them for the benefit of his school and brighter pupils. One of these men, Adam Martindale, forbidden by the Five Mile Act of 1665 to teach within five miles of a city or corporate town, came to teach mathematics in Manchester. 'I had much encouragement from Mr Wickens, Master of the Free School,' he recalled, 'who sent me a good number of his most ingenious boys and admired their great proficiency.' In 1667 it was Wickens who persuaded Adam Martindale that his son was ripe for Cambridge.

In his letter to the Secretary of State, William Butterworth had descibed Wickens as old and infirm. In fact the High Master was to outlive his former pupil by seven years. In addition, in 1663 he was almost stolen from Manchester by the Haberdashers' Company, who wanted this distinguished master to take over their new school at Newport in Shropshire. When Wickens accepted the invitation, the citizens of Manchester were so dismayed that a large public meeting urged him to reconsider.

One of Wickens' closest companions, Henry Newcombe, formerly master of Congleton Grammar School and formerly the preacher of the Collegiate church, was also determined to keep his friend in Manchester. Newcombe's anxieties were made all the greater since, like many Mancunians, he disliked the Grammar School usher, an inadequate teacher named Samuel Birch, and feared he might succeed his friend as High Master.

But he fought valiantly for Wickens. Newcombe first decided to approach a leading feoffee to persuade him to rally his fellow feoffees to the cause of keeping Wickens. He chose Lord Delamere, formerly Sir George Booth of Dunham Massey, a Presbyterian who in 1659 had helped to organise a rising in favour of Charles II, and Lord Delamere promised his help. Next Newcombe wrote to the Haberdashers' Company, asking them to relinquish their claim on Wickens. Finally, throughout the latter half of July and the beginning of August, Newcombe, as his diary records, met frequently with John Wickens, continually pressing him to remain at the Manchester Grammar School. In the end Wickens deferred to this pressure, graciously accepting an increase in salary and a larger house, which was capacious enough to accommodate paying boarders and thus bring him yet more money.

Penelope Wickens died in December 1685, cared for in her last illness by Henry Newcombe's wife. When John Wickens himself died in 1676, the president of Corpus Christi College, Oxford, appointed one of his own fellows, Daniel Hill, as High Master. A year later Hill had resigned, and was replaced by Hugh Barrow, head master of Preston Grammar School, born in

*A baby owl finds an apt perch on the school's statue of Hugh Oldham.*

Lancaster and educated both at St Alban's Hall and Corpus Christi College, Oxford. Barrow had known the Wickens family well enough to marry Isobel, the daughter of John and Penelope Wickens. Barrow remained High Master for an astonishing forty-three years, assisted for twenty-six of them by Richard Thompson, usher from 1696–1721.

Barrow's discipline broke down at least once to our knowledge. Around the year 1690 the boys and masters disagreed violently about the length of the Christmas holiday. Locking themselves in the school and locking the masters out, the boys secured the support of some townspeople, who supplied them with both victuals and beds, which they put in through the school windows. Some townsfolk even supplied the boys with firearms and ammunition, enabling them to fire at the legs of anyone who tried to get inside the school. The rebellion lasted about a fortnight, as its chronicler notes 'somewhat to the disgrace of those who ought to have exerted a better discipline'.

Younger boys were now being admitted to the school (taught in what became known as the Petit School), and by 1685 an extra master to care for them joined the High Master and usher. He was paid only £12 per annum, whereas Barrow received £60 and Thompson £28. Their salaries – at least Barrow's and Thompson's – were augmented by gratuities: £5 for the High Master and £1.10s for the usher in 1685; £10 for the High Master and £2 for the usher in the following two years. In 1690 the master of the Petit School got a rise, and all the gratuity of all three masters in 1690 was a generous £20.

In spite of occasional acts of indiscipline and the High Master's increasingly fragile health towards the end of his regime (when the school solicitor, Edward Hulton, a man of scarcely twenty-three years, ran the whole school, acting as High Master, usher and master of the Petit School), the Manchester Grammar School under William Barrow managed to uphold the high standards that had been achieved during the Commonwealth and Protectorate. The ability of this school (and other grammar schools too) to send poor boys to university was considerably aided by the generosity of the rich, twice-widowed Dowager Duchess of Somerset. Her first husband had been educated at Brasenose College and her second husband had bestowed some of their wealth on that same Oxford house. In 1679 the Duchess set aside profits of the manor of Iver in Buckinghamshire for seven years, to maintain four scholars from Manchester Free School at Brasenose. As the Latin inscription on her tomb in Westminster Abbey rightly has it, her aim was 'to promote the welfare of young men of excellent promise, piety and learning.' She particularly specified that her preferred scholars should be drawn from the counties of Lancashire, Cheshire and Hereford.

Three years later the Duchess married Henry Hare, Lord Coleraine. She was possessed of too independent a temper for his taste. They soon lived apart by mutual consent, and she devoted herself to further charitable works, in particular to drawing up a will in 1686 which created scholarships at both Brasenose College, Oxford and St John's College, Cambridge, to support poor scholars from Hereford School, Marlborough, and the Manchester

*The tomb in Westminster Abbey of the Duchess of Somerset, patroness of 'young men of excellent promise, piety and learning' from Manchester Free School.*

Grammar School. One of the three trustees of these scholarships was the Earl of Warrington, formerly Lord Delamere and still a feoffee of the school. Somehow Manchester Grammar School managed to grab most of the scholarships for its own pupils.

A similar bonus to the school was provided by one of the Duchess' contemporaries, William Hulme of Kersley, who had been one of Nehemiah Painter's pupils and went on from the Grammar School to Brasenose. One of his close friends noted how he observed 'that the county of Lancaster, especially about Manchester, had sent more scholars to the University than any like county or place, but that many who sent their sons were not able to maintain them any longer than to make them Bachelors of Arts.' Hulme determined to remedy this. He was astutely reacting to a change in the habits of the university.

Until the Restoration most students stayed at Oxford for seven years, taking the Bachelor of Arts degree after four and their MA three years later. Now many students began to leave once they had taken their BA. When Hulme died in 1691, his will provided for four young men 'of the poorest sort' to be maintained for four more years at Brasenose College after they had taken their BA degrees, all four to be nominated by the warden of the Collegiate church and the rectors of Bury and Prestwich.

Such generosity apparently inspired the feoffees to match it, and in the early eighteenth century we find them frequently granting money to former scholars who were now at university. Their accounts also reveal that with equal frequency they treated themselves to ample dinners.

To succeed such a man as Hugh Barrow who had been High Master for so long was a task to which Thomas Colburn proved unequal. He failed even to attract a competent usher and resigned within two years of his appointment. His successor, John Richards, proved a complete disaster.

For a start he was rarely in the school. Inevitably parents began to withdraw their children and prospective parents looked elsewhere. Next he had, through no fault of his own, inherited a master named Seth Broxup who, though only sixty-eight, was no longer fit to run the Petit School. Third, Richards could not attract and keep masters competent enough to look after the Petit School.

In 1724 the feoffees, donating gratuities of £25 to the High Master, £13 to his usher (a man named Purnell to whom the school was to be enormously indebted) and £3 to Seth Broxup, added the rider 'That Mr Broxup by reason of his insufficiency, to forthwith quit the School.' Broxup, who had taught at the Grammar School since 1688 and admitted that he was beginning to feel himself in decline, was nevertheless astounded. As he wrote to the feoffees, 'hearing you had a design of displacing me, it was surprising and amazing to me and I was almost sunk down with horror and despondency, but my sorrow was soon alleviated when Mr Richards informed me you would continue me in my place until the 25th March next ensuing, which comfortable news brought great security to my mind and filled me with transports of joy.' In fact the feoffees had already appointed his successor, a man named Joseph Hobson who had not even been to university. Hobson found himself in charge of eighty-six children, including girls, aged between five and twelve.

After five years the feoffees turned against the High Master. First they asked their lawyer to enquire what were their rights in increasing or decreasing the salaries of the masters according to their abilities. They demanded next 'what are the proper methods to proceed against the masters in case they neglect the School and still insist upon having and enjoying all the Revenues.' Finally, attacking his 'gross negligence' and absence from the school, they determined to reduce John Richards' salary from £60 to £10 a year. By 1727 Richards had quit his post.

He had apparently been ill, for the feoffees in 1731 paid his successor £160, Mr Purnell £50, two other masters (Mr Hobson and Mr Gore) £20 each, and a Mr Arrowsmith £10 'for assisting in the schoole during Mr Richards' illness.' The following year Gore, the writing master, was given the stark option of accepting only £12 a year or resigning. Purnell, by contrast, was offered £10 in lieu of a house. Gore apparently chose to resign, for in 1737 a new writing master, Robert Lowe, appears, paid £20 a year to teach the Petit School. In the meantime a couple of pupil teachers in the Petit School had been each paid £5 for a year's work.

The new High Master was Henry Brooke, a former scholar of the Grammar School and a fellow of Oriel College, Oxford. A learned man, who had already published editions of the classics, he was to create for the feoffees as many problems as Richards. Yet he had winning gifts, once writing a poem called 'The Quack Doctor' which he declaimed to the whole school. One of his pupils praised him as 'an accurate and accomplished scholar, though lenient as a disciplinarian'.

Initially, he certainly seemed to be a man with the interests of the boys at heart. Brooke began to write a history of the school, though he never finished it. He also started a register of admissions, so that for the first time we know the names of all those who came to the Manchester Grammar School and what sort of boys they were. The very first entry, for example, names Thomas Coppock and identifies him as the son of John Coppock, a Manchester taylor. Thomas Coppock went on to Brasenose from the school, took his BA in 1742, was ordained and in 1745 allied himself with Bonnie Prince Charlie. He was made chaplain to the Manchester Regiment. The Jacobite insurrection failed, and the following year Coppock was hanged at Harrowby gallows near Carlisle. A similar, though not quite so drastic, fate awaited another scholar, William Brettargh, the son of a Leigh attorney, who entered the school on 13 January 1734. He too joined Charles Stuart's insurrection, and his fate was to be conveyed from Southwark gaol to Gravesend, whence he was transported for life.

From the number of entries in the register we can calculate that at this time the school consisted of some 120 boys. Only four came from outside Manchester and Salford – two from Leigh, one from Whitchurch and one from Middleton. None of the early entries records a boy who was the son of a gentleman. The fathers of the Manchester Grammar School boys were tailors, innkeepers, hatters, joiners, tradesmen, glaziers, corn merchants and the like. An exception was the attorney's son, the transported William Brettargh. The Revd Joseph Downes, chaplain of the Collegiate church, sent his son Charles

35

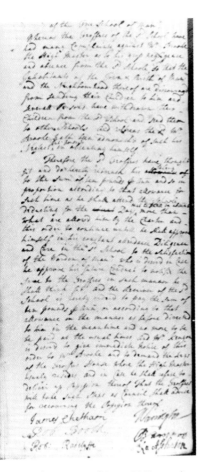

*The minute of June 1743 recording the decision of the foeffees to reduce the salary of the High Master.*

to the school in 1735. The entries for 1736–7 include the sons of an innkeeper, a writing master, a fustian-man, a calendar man, a tradesman and then the 'son of Joseph Yates of Manchester, esquire', a boy who became a judge in the court of the King's Bench.

Brooke's salary was increased to £200 a year. Soon, however, the number of entrants to the school began to decline alarmingly. In 1735 only six boys entered the school, in 1741 only nine, in 1742 only eight and in 1743 only five. Like his predecessor John Richards, Henry Brooke had grown weary of the school and was hardly ever there. In February 1741 the feoffees stopped paying him 'for his gross non-attendance of the school' and shut him out of the High Master's house in Long Millgate. The effect of their action made little difference to Brooke's lax behaviour. In June 1743 the feoffees felt obliged to reduce his annual salary from £200 to the founder's original stipulation of £10. Their minutes for 1744 record that they paid Mr Purnell 30 guineas 'for teaching the Upper School 30 weeks, in the absence of Mr Brooke, the High Master.'

At last Brooke was stirred into action. He published a defence of himself in 1744, addressed to the warden of the Collegiate church and the feoffees, which constitutes both his own creed as a teacher and a statement of how he saw the role of the Manchester Grammar School.

First, as an Anglican he rejected what he described as the 'Popish' religious provisions of the founder. Instead he had, he claimed, been accustomed to using the Book of Common Prayer each morning and each evening during the school terms, while endeavouring 'to instil into the minds of the youth all such duties, especially upon which the honour of God and the happiness of mankind chiefly depend.' As for learning, his aim was not simply to teach young people to construe the classics but also to lead them 'by degrees in their Compositions to the imitating of them.'

Finally, the preface to his tract referred to his recent absence from the school, 'upon necessary business' as he claimed. Brooke confessed that at that time 'I had thoughts of quitting the school, and putting in a substitute, as I was informed, with the consent and to the satisfaction of all concerned.' He had changed his mind: 'now being at free liberty, I shall keep close to the school and the business thereof in person, . . . desiring nothing more than the benefit and improvement thereof.'

The rest of Henry Brooke's tract was his address to the school when it broke up for the Christmas holiday in 1744. Although Brooke sometimes used money from the feoffees to furnish the school library with modern literature – such as a copy of Defoe's recently published *Robinson Crusoe, Gulliver's Travels* and eight volumes of *The Spectator* – as well as a French dictionary and Fénelon's *Telemachus* (in an English translation), he remained basically a passionate classicist. His address of 1744 consists of a spirited defence of learning the dead languages of Latin and Greek rather than studying French or the liberal arts and sciences. Brooke believed that no translation could adequately convey the profound thoughts of Latin and Greek originals. He believed the classics to be 'perfect pieces in all sorts of composition; perfect as far as human wit can reach.' They were, he declared, 'the very pictures of nature in her finest array, her greatest glory,' and therefore 'deservedly proposed for our imitation.' Not even the finest writings in English matched them in natural purity, strength, harmony, and simplicity of language.

What is more, Brooke argued, the revival of classical learning, the foundation of grammar schools such as his, the refinement of the English language, the revitalising of Britain and the great blessing of the Reformation had all of them gone hand in hand. 'Before the Reformation, when Classical learning was disused, our language was rough and void of every grace; our thoughts uncouth and unrefined, and a total gloom overspread the whole Nation; but soon after, when the differences and troubles of that time were composed, Grammar Schools being erected to open the minds of the next generation, and show them the errors of the Church of Rome, the Classics were called out of darkness and set at liberty.' So men and women 'entered into a spacious, open field,' their prospects enlarged, new thoughts in their heads and speaking almost a new language.

Thus Brooke's creed involved teaching the classics, allied to the Bible and the Book of Common Prayer, in order, as he put it, 'to maintain the ground upon which we stand' and also to counteract what he discerned as 'the general relaxation, extravagance, and licentiousness' of the time.

Brooke and the feoffees had come to terms. Thenceforth he returned to his duties. The school began to flourish again. The register records that thirty new boys were admitted between March 1744 and March 1745. The feoffees remained cautious. Only in June 1747 did they start paying the High Master again, adding a gratuity of £35 a quarter to his salary. In October of the same year, in view of the fact that he had 'duly attended for the time of 3 years and 9 months', he was given £490 back pay and was promised re-entry to the High Master's house the following May.

In 1749 Brooke retired as High Master, taking the Oriel living of Tortworth in Gloucestershire. He died ten years later, aged sixty-three.

At last the merits of William Purnell were recognised. He had been usher for nearly twenty-six years, having also served as vicar of Unsworth to compensate for his poor salary. He was well-placed (his cousin was warden of New College, Oxford), and was a graduate of Oriel. A charitable man, he had supported the establishment of an infirmary in Manchester and a new parochial school at Newton (where he had become vicar after relinquishing Unsworth). His delight in contemporary literature made some critics maliciously suppose that Henry Brooke's defence of the classics was partly a covert attack on his usher.

The school began to prosper again. Thirty-six new boys, for example, came in 1753. An increasing number of children of the nobility appeared in the school. Boys came from further afield, so that the number of boarders increased, with half of them going on to university. Millington Massey of Durham, admitted in Purnell's first year as High Master, went on to become senior wrangler at Cambridge. Some boys used the Grammar School as a kind of preparatory school for Westminster. Among them Cyril Jackson became Dean of Christ Church, William Jackson Bishop of Oxford, and John Crewe became Lord Crewe.

The new High Master's literary interests can be detected in his additions to the school library. The works of Pope, Smollett and Sheridan, Spenser's *Faerie Queene* and the poems of Matthew Prior now stood shoulder to shoulder with Brooke's editions of the classics. Purnell also expanded an innovation of his predecessor. In Henry Brooke's time the Grammar School boys around Christmas had performed 'scenes' or plays. In 1753 Purnell was so delighted at the opening of Manchester's first theatre that he transferred there the school's annual speech day. Six years later, just before the Christmas holidays, his pupils were performing classical and other plays in the theatre for their parents, relatives and friends.

Ten boys appeared that year in a performance of *Cato*, probably written by Dr John Brown of Newcastle-on-Tyne. The handbill announcing the play decreed that 'No persons will be allowed to go behind the Scenes, or stand upon the stage,' and that 'None was to be admitted without tickets.'

Dr John Byrom professed himself to be outraged by this performance (which, he supposed, encouraged the boys to vice) and wrote anonymously to tell Purnell so. Purnell's reply was splendidly powerful. First he rebuked Byrom for sending his sentiments 'in a disguised manner.' He continued: 'My notions of the stage are different from yours.' Purnell declared that the stage could promote good ends and purposes, virtue and religion, quite as well as

*By 1760, as this 'bird's eye' view reveals, Manchester was fast becoming the largest village in England. The school appears behind Chetham's gateway in the upper lefthand quarter.*

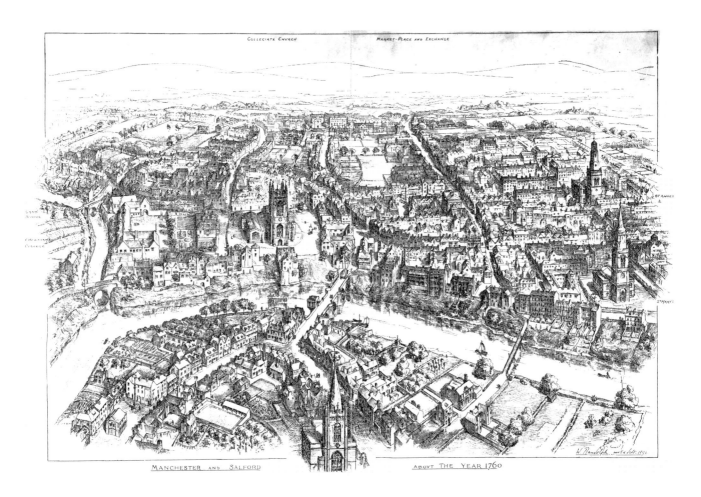

MANCHESTER AND SALFORD    ABOUT THE YEAR 1760

the pulpit. 'I have lately received some sermons from a friend, a doctor in divinity, and some plays from a friend, a doctor in divinity,' Purnell continued; 'and there is more sense, more learning and more religion in the plays than in the sermons.' He further contended that 'There are some vices more fit for the stage than the pulpit.' He insisted that 'If I thought the play would taint the minds of any of my youths, I would never have engaged in it.'

This vigorous self-defence by one of the Manchester Grammar School's most genial High Masters concluded with the words, 'As to virtue and religion, I have as great a regard for them as yourself; but as to reputation, I am entirely indifferent to it. You may publish the epilogue when you please.'

William Purnell insisted that his youths, far from harmed, were 'much benefited' by the play. It is fascinating to follow some of their later careers. Richard Pepper Arden, who played Cato, became Lord Chief Justice of the common pleas, was created Baron Alvanley and made a privy councillor; James Heap, who played Lucius, became Vice-Principal of Brasenose College, Oxford; George Travis, who played Juba, became Archdeacon of Richmond; John Arden, who played Portius, became a feoffee of the school and high sheriff of Cheshire; William Arnold, who played Marcus, graduated as a doctor of divinity and became senior wrangler and sub-praeceptor to the Prince of Wales; George Buckey Bower, who played Marcia, became a fellow of Brasenose and afterwards Archdeacon of Richmond; and Foster Bower, who played Lucia, became recorder of Chester.

Undeterred by Byrom's criticism, the High Master arranged for a second performance of *Cato* in 1761. The eloquence which Richard Arden (who again played Cato) was later to need in his adult life was already apparent, fostered in part by Purnell's love of the theatre. In 1761 he recited a prologue to the play, saying as much:

> It has been often, and too truly, said,
> That men train'd up in schools and deeply read,
> When summon'd out to tread the world's great stage,
> And in the scenes of public life engage,
> Unskill'd, and awkward, scarce are ever brought
> Justly to speak what they so well have thought;
> But with ungraceful gesture, abject fear,
> Or tone offensive to the nicer ear,
> Disgrace the subject which they should adorn,
> And 'stead of praise are heard only with scorn.
>   To shun the rock on which so many split,
> Which renders learning dull, and tasteless, wit;
> We thus presume to tread the buskin'd stage,
> And risk attempts so far beyond our age.
> The motive sure is good; excuse it then
> If boys, who hope in time to act like men,
> Leave for awhile their Latin and their Greek,
> And their own native English learn to speak;

Learn to speak well what well they hope to write,
And manly eloquence with truth unite.

The voice was Arden's; the sentiments were Purnell's. But perhaps the future chief justice penned them himself, for he was later to display a droll wit in writing verse. Arden once wrote some lines to a rich lady who lived by the celebrated spa at Buxton, asking her to give money for some poor invalids:

> Gentle lady, pray be kind
> To the halt, the lame, the blind,
> Who came to Buxton from a distance,
> And cannot, without your assistance,
> Afford so long to bathe, and drink,
> As they and the physicians think
> Would be of service to their bodies –
> Then don't refuse, O lovely goddess!
> To give a little boon, I beg,
> That he, who had a wooden leg,
> May get such strength into the other,
> That it may scarcely want its brother;
> And she who has a single eye
> May keep it open till she die;
> So he, who ne'er can hope to dance,
> May here at least be made to prance;
> And she, who cannot kill her man,
> May see the eyes of you who can,

verses redeemed from the description of doggerel not solely by their wit but also by the audaciously covert proposition in the last two lines.

On 16 April 1764 William Purnell died, still in office and aged only sixty-three. In death he proved as charitable as in life, leaving part of his property to support the new Manchester Infirmary and £200 to the school at Newton, to pay for the free education of fifteen poor children. He had served the Manchester Grammar School for forty-one years.

PLATE 3

*Left: Detail from a portrait of Charles Lawson now hanging in the school hall.*

*Right: The oldest surviving fragment of the school is the cast iron owl from the front of 1776 school building, Lawson's school.*

*Below: The second Grammar School building, abutting onto the fifteenth century building which became Chetham's Hospital. Note the owl peeping from the gable end.*

PLATE 4

*By the end of the eighteenth century Long Millgate and the surrounding area were becoming increasingly insalubrious. The feoffees noted that both the High Master's House and the usher's house in which most scholars boarded were 'closely surrounded by Old Buildings chiefly occupied by poor people, in situations neither healthy nor comfortable.' Lawson's house at the beginning of the nineteenth century.*

*Houses in Manchester's Gibraltar area, close to Long Millgate (an early nineteenth century drawing).*

# 3

## Al Fine? Or the School in Peril
### 1764–1859

'OUR founders,' averred William Purnell's successor as High Master, 'were men who lived not in shade and retirement, but in the most illustrious scenes of public life; who served their country in the highest offices of church and state.' His own aim was to take boys into his school and kindle in them the same ardour for high office. For a time he succeeded. So, for a time, did his sucessors.

In 1749, at the tender age of 22, Charles Lawson had been appointed William Purnell's usher. Lawson was a native of Lincolshire, and came with an excellent reference from the head of his Oxford college (Corpus Christi) and another from a fellow Oxonian, a Mancunian named Robert Thyer, who described the new usher as 'a very modest, pretty sort of young man,' who 'will set about retrieving the character of the School.'

Lawson, the son of a Lincolnshire clergyman, though ordained a deacon in the Anglican church, never became a priest. That would have involvced swearing an oath of allegiance to King George II, and Lawson was sufficiently devoted to the cause of the Jacobites to refuse.

He and Purnell perfectly complemented each other, the latter pursuing his love of contemporary literature with the boys of his school while Lawson taught them classics and mathematics. Fifteen years after his appointment, on the death of Purnell, it was virtually inevitable that Lawson be appointed his successor.

In his prime Charles Lawson was no mean figure. On taking up office as High Master he spoke at length of 'the important duty which I have, perhaps, too rashly undertaken to discharge.' Public schools were once again under attack. Lawson referred to the accusation that public schools endanger the morality of young persons, pointing out in defence that 'it may, upon experience, be found less difficult to preserve children from the contagion of vicious servants at home, than from that of loose companions abroad.' Next he countered the suggestion that because each teacher had such a great number of pupils under his care, scarcely one of the boys could be given individual

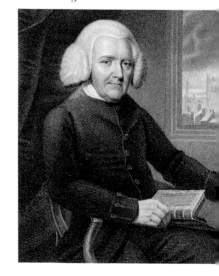

*Charles Lawson, High Master of the Manchester Grammar School 1764–1807, an engraving by J. Thompson from the portrait by W. M. Craig. Lawson holds a volume of Homer's Iliad; the Collegiate Church as well as some of Manchester's crowded dwellings are visible through the window.*

attention by arguing first that no institution is perfect and secondly that in truth the discretion of a good master did enable him to suit his teaching to the different tempers and dispositions of his pupils.

*An 1821 engraving with the school's second building on the right.*

Lawson further insisted that such schools as his prepared boys for the world of business far better than any other upbringing, and he believed that they undoubtedly contrived to 'shake off that unmanly weakness with which the ill-judged fondness of parents is apt to enervate the mind.' And above all such schools as his provoked in boys the desire to emulate the best of their companions. 'That children are not destitute of this powerful incentive is very certain,' Lawson asserted: 'the sparks of this ardour are latent in their breasts, and they can be no where so effectually kindled into a flame as in a Public School.' So, Lawson argued, ''Tis here, and not in the privacy of a domestic education, that this principle displays itself in full force, and urges the generous mind to the utmost exertion of all its faculties: What hopes may we not entertain of a youth inspired by this active flame? What heights can we conceiving him incapable of attaining?'

Lawson had developed some of those personal quirks which endear schoolmasters to their pupils. One was to address everyone in the third person, beginning with the phrase 'Psha, blockhead.' Deep down he was exceedingly kind. A Bishop of Chichester who had been his pupil used to pass the Whitsuntide and Christmas holidays with his aunt and uncle who lived near Gisburn in Yorkshire. His uncle never allowed his horses to sleep away from their own stables, so he told the boy that he would send a coach to pick him up only as far as Haslingden. The boy would have to find his own way there.

As the first school holiday approached, Lawson asked the boy in his oblique fashion, 'Psha, blockhead, pray where does he go these holidays?' The boy told him of the arrangement with his uncle and aunt. 'And how is he to get to Haslingden?' asked the High Master. 'That I should walk,' came the answer. 'Well, pray then, can he ride?' asked Lawson, and being told yes, said, 'Psha, well then, he shall have my horses to Haslingden.' Lawson kept his promise to the lad so long as he remained at school. 'Have I not reason to revere and love his memory?' the Bishop exclaimed after his old High Master's death.

Lawson's early years running the school were years of achievement. His predecessor's academic successes were repeated, and initially the school continued to flourish. By 1770 the number of boys had increased from 100 to around 150, many of them boarders, so that in 1775 he was obliged to appoint another assistant, the Revd James Pedley. By 1784, 183 of the boys taught under Lawson's regime had gone on to university, where most of them shone.

Manchester, though still technically a town and not a city, was now undergoing a remarkable growth. By 1800 it had doubled in size since Lawson became High Master of its Grammar School, and now boasted a population of 84,000. In that year Thomas de Quincy entered the school. Lawson was now over seventy years old. He had probably clung on to his office too long. Forty years later de Quincy recalled his time at the school with some asperity, for he had been so miserable there that he ran away after eighteen months. For a start de Quincy disliked the upper schoolroom, an immense building ninety-six feet long and thirty-six feet wide, with a ceiling between twenty and thirty feet high. De Quincy judged that 'though of ample proportions the room was

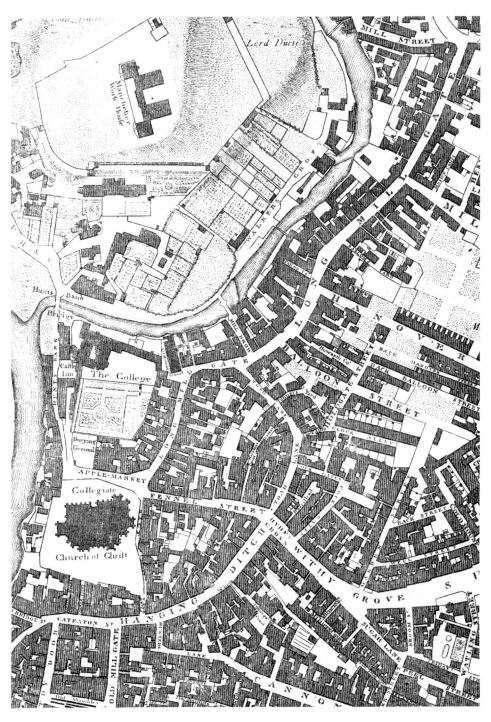

*Extract from William Green's large scale map of Manchester (1787–94). The environment of the school was becoming increasingly built up and squalid.*

dreary', and he complained that 'the external walls, which might have been easily and at little expense adorned with scenes from classic history, were quite bare.' In his recollection, 'nothing relieved the monotony'.

Unhappy memories may well have warped de Quincy's reminiscences. He

44

mocked the way Lawson would hold a daily roll-call in the inner courtyard of his house as if it were an Oxford quad with himself as master of an Oxford college. He smirked at the way Lawson generously provided his groom with a hunter and a horse, since the groom rarely used them. He refused even to visit the lower, 'plebeian' school as he dubbed it, which had been founded in 1685 to prepare boys for the Grammar School proper and where younger boys were taught 'the lowest mechanical accomplishments of reading and writing' by an English master, the Revd John Gaskell.

One of de Quincy's near contemporaries at the school, the radical Samuel Bamford, gave a different picture, describing lower school as 'a large room of an oblong form extending north and south, and well lighted by large windows,' warmed at the northern end by a fireplace 'with a cheerful fire glowing in the grate.' The master's custom, Bamford continues, 'was to sit in an armchair with his right hand towards the fire and his left arm resting on a square oaken table, on which lay a newspaper or two, a magazine or other publication, a couple of canes with the ends split, and a medley of boys' playthings, such as tops, whips, marbles, apple-scrapers, nutcrackers, dragon banding and such articles.' And just as Lawson had developed a reputation as 'Long Millgate's flogging Turk,' so Gaskell would readily cane boys who were late or caught fighting and playing with tops and balls when they should have been working.

Gaskell had other peculiarities. Another pupil remembered him as 'rubicund, dignified and reserved, speaking little and not to be spoken to by the boys, as that would have proved a serious interruption to the important business in which he was for the most part engaged, perusing pamphlets and pruning the pimples which profusely decorated his chin.' No one was allowed to speak to him, so that when a boy wished to leave the room he would circle round his desk, maintaining a respectful distance, keeping continually on the move, ceaselessly bobbing his head until the English master looked up and gave a curt nod. As for the usher's assistant, the Revd George Holt, he was described as 'an immensely tall, lank and lathy person, with a corresponding longitude of arm, which enabled him to wield the cane with powerful effect, a talent which he did not suffer to lie dormant.'

Charles Lawson's school was divided into six classes. Work began at seven o'clock, and Lawson would frequently carry on teaching after nine o'clock, even though the boys were expected to breakfast then, finishing in time to start work again at half past nine. At noon study ceased for three hours, after which the boys were again taught until five. Holidays were lengthy – though not so lengthy as in today's schools – with five weeks in summer and around Christmas, as well as breaks at Shrovetide and Easter. Shrove Tuesday was marked by a competition with bows and arrows, ending in a feast at the Bull's Head Inn.

Of the six classes, one studied the elements of Latin, three studied the Bible in various depths, a fourth was taught the New Testament, and two more learned how to spell. Each class sat on strong, oaken benches, and the last two groups ('considered as children among the boys,' according to Bamford) were the only ones without desks.

By contrast with this approving description of the school's facilities, de Quincy's unflattering portrait of the school at the turn of the century extended to lamenting its lack of a playground (though he conceded that it may have 'added to our sense of dignity by keeping the boys exclusive'), to speculating about Lawson's private life 'he had known the pangs of unrequited affection', and to complaining that in his years as a pupil Lawson complimented him only once, for successfully translating one of Steele's *Spectator* essays into Latin.

When he began to board in the High Master's own house de Quincy grew even more morose, for the bad weather and parting from friends depressed him. Then the volatile youth perked up again, for his schoolfellows welcomed him ardently. On his first evening as a boarder with Lawson he admired the way his fellow pupils, discussing the arguments for the truth of Christianity as set forth by Grotius, were perfectly willing and able to disagree with the views of the seventeenth century philospher.

Yet however cautiously we accept de Quincy's memoir, by now Lawson was becoming less successful, and his school began to attract fewer pupils, in consequence sending fewer to Oxford and Cambridge. In part this was simply the result of the increasingly advanced age of the High Master and his usher, the Revd John Darby, who, like Lawson, had been appointed in 1764. If his pupils are to be believed, Darby was no great schoolmaster, 'silky' and 'a fellow whose words were as mellifluous, as his heart was devoid of feeling,' in addition to being 'by no means highly qualified for the responsible figure he then occupied in the school,' and completely failing to win the affections or command the respect of the boys. As for Lawson, de Quincy judged that 'Life was over with him, for its hopes and and for its trials.' The one trial remaining was to fight against a painful malady; and said de Quincey, 'He still had his dying to do.'

As another pupil recalled, by this time Lawson had become 'a personage of most venerable aspect – an old, old man, apparently on the extreme verge of life.' He described the High Master as wearing a complete suit of black velvet, lace ruffles at his wrist and diamond buckles on his shoes, 'with a well-powdered Peruque projecting, like a full-blown cauliflower from behind.' As this former pupil remembered, the aged High Master used to enter the school with feeble, tottering steps as if about to fall, and fall at length he did, and either died on the spot or was carried home in a dying state. The year was 1807.

Inevitably, run by such old men as Lawson and Darby, the school had begun to decline. In the early 1780s some sixty boys enrolled each year. In the early 1800s the number fell to barely twenty. The teaching methods were moribund. When Frederick Baltimore Calvert, a son of the Duke of Norfolk's Glossop steward, entered the school in 1804, he found himself and his fellows being taught Latin day by day by rote thus (as he remembered at the age of eighty) 'without understanding one syllable of what we were repeating.' Calvert's lament continues:

Nothing was explained to us: Even such words as nominative, genitive, dative, indicative, potential, subjunctive were left to our own ingenuity to discover, stimulated only by the powerful inculcation of the cane; for everything was thrashed into us, not by the laws, but by such unsparing application of the above instrument to our backs and shoulders, that they were never without a regular succession of discolorations, displaying when uncovered every gradation of bruise, from the black mark left by the recent stroke of the cane, to the convalescent stages of green and yellow; nor had this cruel scourging any thing to do with our demerits; it depended entirely on the humour our master happened to be in, and we used anxiously to watch his face in a morning, to judge by the expression whether it was to be a quiet or a caning day.

Such experience, he declared, breaking down his youthful buoyant spirit and extinguishing the early sunshine of life, had 'converted the lightheartedness of the boy into a load more difficult to bear, than the burden of four score.'

In part this decline under Lawson was also due to the changing demography of Manchester and its environs, with a new and large industrial class cut off from the rest of society and a merchant class increasingly clamouring for an education in modern languages and science, neither of which the Manchester Grammar School was as yet offering (though Lawson had been augmenting his income by teaching mathematics privately since the 1750s, and in the 1780s began teaching it to his boarders for a fee). In the perspicacious words of one of Lawson's obituaries, the school had for some years past considerably diminished in the number of its members 'from a peculiarity of local disadvantages'.

The feoffees also noted that Long Millgate was becoming increasingly insalubrious, so much so that in 1808 they were contemplating moving the school to a site out of town. Both the High Master's house and the usher's, in which most scholars boarded, were, the feoffees noted, 'closely surrounded by Old Buildings chiefly occupied by poor people, in situations neither healthy or comfortable.' Since Long Millgate was the site of Manchester's thrice weekly apple market, it was frequently crowded with horses and carts, making it difficult for the boys to cross from the masters' houses to the school. In the absence of a playground, the boys spent their free time in the neighbouring streets, and were subjected to unsavoury temptations. 'The resorting to taverns and intercourse with women of the town becomes a fashion amongst the Boys in the higher classes of the school, which no vigilance of the masters can suppress,' the feoffees lamented. 'All this makes a serious impression upon the minds of those parents who live at a distance, with the result that for several years the number of scholars has declined.'

Lawson's successor as High Master grappled with these problems for the next thirty years. The Revd Jeremiah Smith had been educated at Hertford College, Oxford, and then took livings around Birmingham while teaching for fourteen years as assistant and then second master at King Edward's School there. He continued the same habits at Manchester, holding livings in Cheetham Hill, Carrington, Salford and Manchester, some of them simultaneously, as well as for some time drawing a salary from the living of Great

*A contemporary engraving of Jeremiah Smith, Jacobite, Tory, and High Master from 1807 to 1837.*

Wilbraham near Cambridge.

'A spare man with large thoughtful features and a fine expansive forehead powdered at the top' (as his pupil Harrison Ainsworth described him), Smith was a good scholar. He looked like a bishop and in Ainsworth's opinion should have been one. 'His voice was particularly solemn and it was quite a treat to hear him read prayers.' Jeremiah Smith could keep boys in order without beating them, and he is reputed to have used the cane only once in his career at Manchester. 'Dignified in manner and deportment, and ever preserving an air of grave courtesy, it would have been impossible to take a liberty with him and it was never attempted,' witnessed Ainsworth.

Once more the roll of boys increased. At the beginning of the nineteenth century Oxford University had reformed its system of public examinations and pupil admissions, and Smith was quick to take advantage of this. His success attracted more and more talented boarders whose parents were equally anxious to exploit the new opportunities. In 1833 the feoffees were enlightened enough to petition the court of chancery to add English, French, German and chemistry to the official curriculum of the school. Three years later they resolved to pay a mathematics and an English master £200 each, a teacher of French and German £150 and a writing master £100. The feoffees set aside a further £50 to buy lexicons in the various foreign languages for the school library, as well as more money to pay a science teacher and buy his equipment.

Jeremiah Smith retired the following year with a handsome pension. This act of generosity on the feoffees' behalf was made possible by one of the school's most ingenious receivers, a man named Josiah Twyford, who had reorganised the mills endowed by the founder. Twyford had pulled down the old mills and built new ones, thereby considerably increasing the revenue. When Smith first arrived in Manchester he feared he would have to divert the River Irk through Lawson's dilapidated and filthy house if he were ever to get it clean. In a scarcely veiled reference to his predecessor Smith declared of his house's many inconveniences, 'I shall never cease to wonder how any feeling and rational creature should have so long acquiesced in them.' With Twyford's help it was soon transformed into what Smith himself described as 'an admirable house'.

In 1818 the usher was given an annual allowance of £84, to enable him to rent a house big enough to house himself and up to thirty boarders. By 1825 Twyford's financial skills had made so much money for the school that the feoffees were able to build a completely new home for the High Master and his ever-increasing number of boarders.

Smith's new boarding house cost £4,450, and an extension to the school another £2,600. Yet envious eyes were being cast on this wealth and the school's successes. Smith's three successors as High Master, Robinson Elsdale, John William Richards and Nicholas Germon, were soon exposed to their hostile glare. For many years the school accounts had been a closely guarded secret, but in 1826 the Charity Commissioners had revealed that the feoffees not only made money but also disposed of a tidy surplus.

If Lawson had been a Jacobite, Smith was a Tory through and through, willing to give evidence against Orator Hunt after Peterloo and signing the petition against the Reform Bill of 1832. His feoffees shared the same political outlook. But much of Manchester and Lancashire was now powerfully behind the Whig party, reformist and intent among other things on promoting elementary education in the county. Though passionately devoted to educating the poor, these Whigs were equally loth to pay for their ideals, and in consequence the opportunities of seizing the endowments of the Manchester Grammar School greatly tempted them. On 15 February 1833 one of their number, a Manchester merchant named Richard Potter who had replaced a Tory old boy of the school as Member of Parliament for Wigan, presented to the House of Commons a petition from the Unitarian congregation of Greengate, Salford, praying the members to take measures to promote a national system of education.

According to *Hansard*, the petitioners expressed their conviction that ample funds might be provided for this purpose from the numerous charitable bequests which had been left for the promotion of education, 'many of which were much mismanaged, to say the least.' Although, were an educational tax imposed, the petitioners declared that they would cheerfully pay their due part, they were convinced that no such tax was necessary. Among the many rich, 'shamefully mismanaged' private charities designed to educate the poor and labouring classes rather than a sect, was that of the Manchester Grammar School.

At the time, the petitioners argued, over £4,400 educated only 150 boys, whereas 'If the bequest were properly managed, instead of 150 boys receiving education, at least 3,000 might be taught.' In addition, they alleged, 'The bequest deed provided that education should not be confined to Latin and Greek.' Supporting the petition in parliament, Mr Wilks again accused the Grammar School of supporting 'great abuses'. He too, though endorsing an extension of education to the poor, wanted this to be paid for by someone else, arguing that 'Ample funds existed for national education, without imposing any additional charge upon the people.' His seconder in the Commons, Mr Brotherton, was equally adamant that their aims could be achieved without any extra financial burden, observing that 'Taxes produced poverty, and poverty produced crime.' According to returns made to parliament, Mr Brotherton said, the annual revenue of endowed schools in England amounted to upwards of £3 million. He concluded that, 'If the unappropriated income of the Manchester Free School, which his honourable friend had alluded to, were judiciously managed, a sufficient provision might be made for the education of a considerable portion of the labouring population of Manchester.'

Under the pseudonym 'A Friend of Popular Education', the Revd Dr J. Relly Beard, minister of Greengate Unitarian Church, published a scathing pamphlet entitled *The Abuses of Manchester Free Grammar School*. His philosophy was totally opposed to the teaching of Latin, an out-dated discipline in his view that long should have been replaced with more useful

49

sciences. Holding that the Manchester Grammar School had alienated money destined for the poor of Manchester and given it to the sons of clergymen and others living outside the boundaries of the town, he now proposed that at least £2,000 of its annual revenues be devoted to new elementary schools.

Equally anonymously, the High Master replied, under the pseudonym 'A Friend of Enlightened Education'. His pamphlet was called *The Abuses of Self-Constituted Authority*, and he vigorously pointed out that Hugh Oldham's foundation had been constituted not solely for the poor but indiscriminately for all children; that it was not confined to the boundaries of Manchester; and that his teachers were splendid.

Robinson Elsdale had demolished the arguments of Dr Beard. But the battle to take away the school's endowments had also been taken up by the new MP for Manchester, Mark Philips. The adroitness of the feoffees in establishing a commercial school in 1833 and 1834 and setting up new buildings for it foiled Philips' attempt to destroy the old classical education completely, for the school could now rightly claim to be serving the needs of the age as well as respecting the wishes of the founder. But Mark Philips and other Manchester Whigs spotted that – contrary to the founder's stipulations – for centuries many of the feoffees of the school had been appointed from outside Manchester. In 1836 some of these Whigs petitioned the Court of Chancery to have the present feoffees removed from office on the grounds of their ineligibility.

Throughout the first two decades of this quarrel Elsdale and his usher John William Richards tried despairingly to educate the childen and boys in their care. In 1839 the Whig Lord Cottenham, who now dominated chancery, had aimed a new blow at the school by decreeing that no surplus funds should be devoted by the feoffees to building any boarding houses for the masters or to supporting any old boy at university.

Robinson Elsdale's health was increasingly precarious and he now applied for and was granted a year's leave of absence. His usher took over, and when at Christmas the ailing Elsdale resigned Richards succeeded him as High Master. He re-instituted annual speech days, which had lapsed in 1830, vainly trying to instil a note of hope into a beleaguered school. Scarcely a year had passed before he lost hope and resigned. His successor was the Revd Nicholas Germon, a teacher at the school since 1825.

Germon was tall and austere, his face close-shaven, his movements dignified and deliberate. He was remembered as a stern and imposing personage, who rarely noticed the younger boys save when the perpetual hum of the schoolroom rose above its normal diapason at which Germon would utter a sonorous 'Silence!' At bottom the boys perceived his kind heart. 'Often in the very heat and whirlwind of his censure his hand, as if by an involuntary impulse of good nature, would steal forth to pat the head or caress the cheek of the trembling little culprit, as who should say, "There, there, my dear! I'm obliged to be very stern, you know, for the sake of discipline; but don't take it too deeply to heart!"'

Fortunately for him and the school the Whig ministry had fallen in 1841, and the new Prime Minister appointed Lord Lyndhurst in place of Lord Cottenham. A Tory and a brilliant scholar, Lyndhurst deplored the notion that the Manchester Grammar School become a purely commercial academy. In his view splitting up education between the leisured and the labouring classes tended only to exacerbate class differences. And he held that 'No system of education was better for the purpose of refining and humanising the manners of a nation than a system of education founded on classical learning.'

Lyndhurst now decreed that Lord Cottenham's decision to prevent boarders being supported by university exhibitions should be set aside and entirely new conditions be determined by the Master in Chancery. Meanwhile the funds of the school, recently the envy of the Manchester radicals, were running dangerously low. An income of over £4,000 in 1849 had dropped within a few years to scarcely £2,500. The mills bequeathed to the school by Hugh Oldham had not always fulfilled his intention of providing his grammar school with a secure income.

The people of the district resented the monopoly and often tried to

*Mills on the River Irk, an early nineteenth century engraving.*

51

circumvent it, for instance by setting up their own mills in Salford and then selling the flour ground there in Manchester. The school lawyers were constantly bringing lawsuits to stop such practices, as well as the sale in Manchester of beer made from malt ground elsewhere.

The school millers were the object of considerable mockery. In 1725 John Byrom wrote a poem warning the two scrawny millers then employed by the school that the town was growing exasperated with their work:

> Here's Bone and Skin, two millers thin,
> Would starve the town or near it,
> But be it known to Skin and Bone,
> That flesh and blood can't bear it.

Nonetheless, even though legal action sometimes seemed near to absorbing most of the profits from their monopoly, the feoffees still defended it.

By the 1750s so much acrimony had arisen over the poor and obsolete state of the school mills that the townspeople tried to have the monopoly abolished by Act of Parliament. In 1758 they partly succeeded. No longer need the citizens use the school's corn mills, and their malt was to be ground henceforth at the fixed price of 1s for six bushels. Unfortunately from the school's point of view, inflation soon began to reduce the value of of this fixed price. As Joseph Aston observed in 1816, by now 'no man could be hired to do the labour of grinding six bushels of malt for one shilling'.

In 1814 the gross profit from the malt mill was £1026.12s 5½d, but when the costs of running it were deducted all the school gained was £300. As we have seen, the appointment of Josiah Twyford as receiver in 1818 led to an improvement. His new, modern corn mills soon began to attract custom away from the other mills inside and outside the town boundaries. But an increasing number of brewers built their premises outside these limits to escape having to grind their malt to the profit of the school. The revenue from the mills, reaching £2,500 in 1833, was less than £400 thirty years later, even though the feoffees had once again tried to increase their efficiency by re-equipping them to be driven by steam power.

To make matters still more precarious for the school, the Liberal party took office again in 1846 and Lord Lyndhurst was replaced by Lord Cottenham. The feoffees openly approached the Master in Chancery with the financial plight. Two years later he made his judgement. In his view boarders should be altogether abolished, and the commercial and classical schools merged into one school, to be known as the Manchester Free Grammar School. A year later Vice-Chancellor Shadwell concurred, and although the feoffees were legally advised to appeal to the House of Lords, they were convinced that their funds could not support such an action.

The main aims of Mark Philips and his fellow radicals in Manchester seem to have been to change the school's curriculum and to eliminate boarders from outside Manchester, many of whom were going on to Oxford and Cambridge at the expense of the school's endowments. He therefore only half-pressed his case over the feoffees, demanding not that all be appointed from persons living in Manchester but that 50 per cent were. When the Court of Chancery finally resolved the dispute in 1849 the feoffees were prevented from using any of their revenues to support boarders going on to university. Once the masters in the old classical school had been paid, the rest of their income was to be spent entirely on the needs of their new commercial school.

The Manchester radicals gleefully proclaimed that 'The object of this suit has been to render a munificent educational charity practically available to the working classes of the inhabitants of Manchester and its vicinity, for whose benefit it was founded.' In fact they had almost succeeded in destroying Hugh Oldham's foundation.

The feoffees now unanimously resigned. The Court of Chancery appointed new ones, all of them 'occupiers of and personally engaged in carrying on business, profession, or other pursuits in manufactories, warehouses, or other establishments in the town or parish of Manchester, and having dwelling houses or places of abode within six miles of the school house.'

Germon spent another ten years as High Master, during which time he was obliged to try to run a school quite different from the one to which he had been appointed. The Manchester Free Grammar School was now obliged to combine educating boys up to eighteen or nineteen who intended to go to university with providing a far more rudimentary education for boys who would leave school at thirteen or fourteen to take up a commercial career. Germon's assistants varied in quality.

Since 1841 the usher had been Richard Thompson, a man of intellectual vigour who at his death left the school library over a thousand volumes. Affectionately known to the boys as Old Tommy, Thompson was an eccentric figure, with 'a rich port-winey complexion,' as a former pupil recalled. He was also extremely short-sighted, though he refused to wear spectacles and habitually surveyed the world through a ponderous, gold-rimmed, square-shaped eye-glass. In consequence he 'could only see a book within three inches of his nose, and the doings of the boys were quite out of his ken.' They took full advantage of this. 'In the intervals between going up to repeat lessons round his desk half the members of a class would slip out and spend the hour or so intended for preparing the next lesson in the playground, secure that their vacant places would never be noticed,' the same ex-pupil tells us; 'nor had they any fears of being unprepared when the lesson time came, for cribs were openly and unblushingly employed beneath his very nose.'

Even less able was the Revd George Slade, who was in charge of the commercial section of the school. Slade taught by rote from textbooks of his own devising, causing a scandal by selling them to the boys for his own profit. The Revd Mr Slade was a married man with children, kindly enough, handsome with black bushy whiskers, though giving the impression 'of an indulgent indifference to his work.'

A boy who had been at the school in 1848 still remembered Slade eighty years later as a kindly man who would 'bite his lips to appease his anger rather than cane a boy.' The same old Mancunian added, 'He was the only master who, as far as my experience goes, took any notice of a boy out of School.' By contrast the new usher, Mr Wadham, possessed an irritable temper. A bachelor who sported long side-whiskers of the style then called 'weepers', Wadham was considered a 'swell'. Inclined to mock the poorer boys whose only fault was their shabby dress, he was nonetheless liked for his ready defence of his own boys, especially when they had been in a fight with the boys of Chetham's College next door.

Yet disillusioned and perhaps also embittered by his experiences, Germon was presiding over a disheartened school, one in his own words 'suffering in the higher divisions from the late discouragements'. Masters are reported to have often slept during school hours. Everyone liberally used the cane – but then, most masters always had done. Although some of the schoolroom walls were covered with maps, no-one ever referred to them. The large and lofty classical school consisted of bare, white-washed walls, lit by two rows of windows and decorated only by a faded escutcheon of the founder at the upper end. No boy was ever set homework. The school examiners continually lamented that because large numbers of boys repeatedly left the classical part of the school, scarcely any of those who replaced them from the elementary school had a decent groundwork in the classics.

In 1855 four masters in the upper school (their desks judiciously placed in front of the four fires which warmed the room in winter) were teaching some seventy boys Latin and Greek. Writing, mathematics and French classes were all considered optional, so few bothered to attend them, for none of the regular masters was present and no-one was responsible for discipline.

In the lower school the same number of boys was taught by one master alone. Mark Philips had long trumpeted that the 1525 foundation deed allowed infants into Hugh Oldham's school, and the decree of 1849 had upheld his view, with the result that these seventy boys were now aged between five and ten. Whereas the masters bizarrely wore their university gowns and the silk top hat of ordinary civil life, Germon had instituted the custom of making boys wear mortar boards, which they continued doing until 1870.

The commercial school (in a separate building) was chaos, with the Revd George Slade vainly attempting to teach English, history, grammar, geography and 'a multitude of other subjects to 150 urchins of 8 to 12 years old'. Slade took one and a half days off each week, when a part-time master came in to teach these urchins writing and accounts. To make matters worse, Germon now had entirely given up running the school and devoted himself to teaching only the top eleven boys in the classical school. Nothing the feoffees or examiners did or said could make him change his ways. As one old Mancunian who entered the school in 1854 remembered, the whole institution 'presented a fair sample of . . . drowsy, lotos-eating apathy.'

One boy's recollection of an incident of this era displays how appallingly discipline had declined as well as the manners of the boys. A little lady with a basket on her arm containing tripe or some such commodity came into the school and complained to the High Master that one of the boys had offended her. Germon told her to walk down the school and point him out. She did so, calling out 'This is him.' The boy got out of his seat, took the little lady and her basket under his arm and carried her out of the school, 'to the great amusement of the whole School and of the masters'.

To such a low ebb had Hugh Oldham's foundation fallen.

The memorial to Charles Lawson erected in 1810 at the entrance to the Manchester Regiment's chapel in the cathedral. Part of the Latin inscription composed by one of his pupils (Dr Frodsham Hodson, Principal of Brasenose College, Oxford, and Vice-Chancellor of the University) reads: 'So scrupulous also was he in the discharge of his duty that neither the weighty cares of business nor the seductions of social recreation – so alluring to an agreeable and witty disposition – could draw him away from his beloved school.'

# 4

## Crescendo

### 1859–1877

'ONE day the whole of the School was thrown into a commotion by the news that the old Germy [Nicholas Germon] had resigned, and that we were to have a brand new Headmaster, straight from Bosphorus [Oxford],' wrote a waggish assistant master at the Manchester Grammar School. 'He was only 27, had been at Rugby, and had brought all the traditions of that great place and of his alma mater with him,' the master continued. 'From the moment of his arrival everything was changed in the School. It began henceforth to compete with the great public schools of England, a hitherto undreamed of ambition filled both master and boys. A pass degree was no longer trumpeted forth as a great event. Essays, Original Latin Verse, Speech Days, Prize Days, even comparative Philology and Sanskrit date from his coming.'

Nicholas Germon had not been easy to dislodge. In 1856 the usher had offered his retirement and the High Master let it be known that he would follow suit if the feoffees could give him a pension of £200 a year. The feoffees replied that he was asking more than their funds could bear. Twice in 1859 Germon repeated his request, mentioning also his failing health, and the second time the feoffees concurred. By the end of April Germon was gone.

Even before Germon's departure the feoffees had been anxiously conferring with Dr Norris, the president of Corpus, about the parlous state of the school and in particular its finances. Dr Norris urged them to petition Chancery to change the scheme which forbade masters to take in boarders or receive capitation fees from boys. While assuring them that he had the best interests of the school at heart, he also declared that to find suitable men to accept the posts of High Master and usher for the low salaries that were being offered would prove difficult.

Nonetheless he managed to appoint a superb High Master, a fellow of his own college. Frederick William Walker was a Londoner of Northern Irish stock, born in Bermondsey in 1830, the son of a hat manufacturer from Tullamore. He had been educated first at St Saviour's Grammar School in Southwark and then at Rugby as a day boy under the regime of Archibald

Campbell Tait, a fellow of Balliol who had left Oxford to succeed Dr Thomas Arnold and was later to become Archbishop of Canterbury. From Rugby, Walker's course was unerringly brilliant: an open scholarship at Corpus Christi College, Oxford, the Vinerian scholarship in Law, the Boden scholarship in Sanskrit and the Tancred scholarship in Law all fell into his grasp. He took a first in moderations and a second in mathematics, and in his finals again took a first in classics and a second in mathematics.

As a philosophy tutor at Corpus he next earned the sobriquet 'malleus philosophorum' from no less an admirer than the formidable Mark Pattison, head of Lincoln College. From Oxford, Walker went to study philology at Dresden. His old headmaster was now Bishop of London, and Tait begged Walker to take holy orders and become his examining chaplain. Instead Walker was admitted a barrister at Lincoln's Inn and joined the western circuit. He proved difficult to deflect from a career at law, at first declining Dr Norris's invitation to go to Manchester and only accepting when Norris called in powerful allies to persuade his protégé.

The opening dialogue when Walker gave evidence to the Taunton Commission in 1865 indicates the man's supreme intellectual self-confidence:

> (*Lord Taunton.*) I believe you are a Fellow of Corpus
> Christi College, Oxford? – I am.
> You took a first class in classics? – Yes.
> You also gained the Sanskrit scholarship? – Yes.
> And the Vinerian scholarship? - Yes.
> I believe you are now the Head Master of the grammar school
> at Manchester? – Yes.

It seemed a natural progression.

Although his effect on the school was entirely beneficial, Walker never quite settled in Manchester. He might easily have done so, for his Nonconformist background made him warm to a feoffee named Richard Johnson who was a deacon at the Union Chapel in Oxford Road. In 1867 Manchester Cathedral witnessed the marriage of the High Master and one of his friend's daughters. Maria Walker bore him a son, whom they named Richard Johnson Walker after her father. Then, following a very short illness she died, leaving to Frederick William Walker her considerable fortune. They had been married for only two years.

A second reason for Walker's frequent restlessness must have been the unremitting hostility to which he was subjected from masters who had grown used to the lax old regime at the Grammmar School and from many Old Mancunians who resented the sweeping changes he made. Nonetheless he imperturbably made the changes. Almost immediately on taking office, Walker made Latin a compulsory subject in the lower school. Parents were horrified. For most of them the lower school was nothing more than an elementary school teaching reading, writing and arithmetic. They had no intention of allowing their sons to learn anything less practical. Worse was to

*A contemporary caricature of Frederick Walker, pens instead of a cigar sprouting from his mouth.*

follow. In 1833 the English school had been created for just such parents, and Walker – entirely ignoring the decree of 1849 – abolished it.

Not only was there an outcry, his action also provoked a great depression in the number of boys entering the school. 'The effect,' he said, 'will not be permanent, I hope.' Precisely what he was aiming at became clear one year after his arrival when the new High Master published the first list of the boys in his school. It presented the Manchester Grammar School as one homogenous body, and one alone. The lower school and the English school had entirely disappeared. Beginning with the lowest form and ending with the sixth formers, Walker simply presented a list of boys. The 'so-called English school', as he pointed out to the feoffees in July 1860, was now decisively linked with the upper school. Already twenty-six boys had passed from it into the upper school.

The list also demonstrated Walker's emphasis on intellectual achievement. The new High Master printed the boys' names in each form rigorously according to their success in the annual exams. Walker had a passion for exams, both internal and external. To his good fortune, in 1860 Manchester became an examining centre for the new Oxford local examinations. Whereas most schools entered, if any boys at all, at most one or two, after an initial year reorganising the Manchester Grammar School Walker entered virtually everyone, some forty boys a year, juniors and seniors alike. They proved to be increasingly successful candidates. In 1863 eighteen passed these exams, five with honours. Five years later forty-four passed, sixteen with honours.

Walker achieved such successes by a decisive transformation of almost every aspect of the school. First he reformed its curriculum. In Germon's time each period had in theory lasted a whole half-day. Walker divided the school week into thirty periods, each an hour long.

Next, whereas Nicholas Germon had become reclusively dedicated to a handful of boys, F. W. Walker tirelessly supervised the whole school. When in 1877 he applied for (and gained) the High Mastership of St Paul's School, London, one of the governors interviewing him asked, 'Well, Mr Walker, what do you do in Manchester?' Walker replied, 'Oh, I just walk around and hear everything.'

In fact Walker himself was clearly an inspired teacher – and certainly no devotee of drudgery. Asked at a public dinner by a leading Manchester merchant why his school did not teach the boys 'the great English classics, Bacon and Locke and David Hume.' Walker paused, and then slowly replied, 'If you had read the books, you would not have asked.' He had two stock questions for the mathematics and science boys. In a maths form he would ask, 'Which is the greater, three-quarters or five-sevenths?' Science classes would be asked, in Walker's deepest tone, 'What can you tell me about the law of Avogadro?' Whatever the reply, Walker listened and said nothing. He gave up asking the first question when a bright boy answered, 'Please, sir, it all depends on the integer.'

Walking around and hearing everything, he soon noticed the inadequacy of some of the masters he had inherited and the unwillingness of some of his own appointees to match his own enthusiasm for work. One of the inherited inadequates was the Revd George Slade, so Walker decided that Slade must go. He was not the only one. Towards the end of 1871 Walker decided that boys who wished to study during the dinner hour should be allowed to stay inside the school buildings, supervised by the masters. Several masters demurred, sending a joint letter to the High Master asking for a 'consultation'. Instead of a consultation they received an ultimatum: those who complied with Walker's new scheme would stay; those who did not would be dismissed.

The Manchester press was outraged. The *Free Lance* published a list of masters alleged to have suffered from Walker's high-handed behaviour. It included:

A. G. Symonds – 'Resigned on being informed that for the last three years he had done his best to injure the school.'
C. C. Sumner – 'Permitted to remain on signing an agreement to quit at a month's notice.'
T. A. Aldis – 'Dismissed. Now one of H.M.'s Inspectors of Schools.'
S. Adair – 'Permitted to remain on signing an agreement to quit at a month's notice.'
E. Lloyd Jones – 'This gentleman would not "peach," and has been dismissed.'
W. M. Watts – 'Dismissed unconditionally.'
L. C. d'Auquier – 'Permitted to remain subject to a month's notice.'

As Walker himself was to say, 'The chief requisite for success is a determined will, without which genius itself is powerless.'

The *Free Lance*, which styled itself 'a Journal of Humour and Criticism,' now attacked Walker under the banner 'The High Hand at the Grammar School', describing the affair as a miserable and undignified squabble which, if allowed to continued, would lead to serious and lamentable consequences for the school. The journal described the dismissed Mr Aldis as a scholar at least the equal of if not superior to Mr Walker. His dismissed colleague Mr Haslam was 'a gentleman of repute.' The *Free Lance* was convinced that in dismissing or rebuking these assistant masters the High Master had acted as a tyrant. 'That an institution so important as the Manchester Grammar School should be handed over to the irresponsible charge of any person – however eminent – is too monstrous a supposition to be for a moment tolerated,' it fulminated. The journal was incensed that Walker was studiously refusing to answer its complaints. 'Gentlemen who have taken honours at their Universities are not likely to accept any such position from which even self-dubbed "professors" might well recoil, nor are the citizens willing to submit their children to the charge of any individual who cannot be called upon to submit the account for the manner in which he performs his duties.'

Apart from Mr Aldis and Mr Haslam, who had no intention of ever entering the school again, all the dismissed or disciplined assistant masters should be reinstated to their former posts and dignity, The *Free Lance* argued. As for the

*A mid-nineteenth century view of the Irk. Manchester was fast becoming a smokey, industrial metropolis.*

High Master, the journal averred that 'Mr Walker is a man of solid attainments and may yet learn the art of governing men and boys without too frequent a display of the birch or the notice to quit.'

F. W. Walker continued serenely on his way. He had his own methods of countering such adverse propaganda. One was to revive the annual speech days, none of which had been held since 1848. At first these were held in the school itself, but in 1872 Walker transferred them to the Free Trade Hall. Each year they proclaimed the achievements of the school. To encourage excellence among both boys and masters, in 1860 he set up an honours board in the school, to record the boys' university successes.

Before his time the school had begun awarding its own prizes for excellence – the Lawson medal, for instance, instituted in 1840 in memory of Charles Lawson, and the Thompson History Prize, endowed by some of Richard Thompson's pupils after his death in 1862. Walker solicited more. The Salford philanthropist and school feoffee Edward R. Langworthy displayed his legendary generosity to the school by giving £10,000 to be invested in order to provide twenty annual scholarships, to be awarded in classics, mathematicss, physical science and modern languages. A subscription in memory of James Lee, the late Bishop of Manchester, raised £200 in 1874, enough to allow Walker to offer yearly prizes to boys who showed exceptional promise at Greek.

The Somerset scholarships at Brasenose and St John's College, Cambridge still remained virtually the sole assistance available for Manchester boys at the ancient universities. The new High Master soon set about supplementing these. In 1870 an old boy and feoffee of the school, Charles Hilditch Rickards,

60

set up a classical scholarship for the school to be held at either Oxford or Cambridge. Two years later Miss Hannah Brackenbury gave debenture stocks in the Lancashire and Yorkshire Railway Company to found exhibitions. In 1874 Philip Wright of Lower Broughton bequeathed £2,440 to Wadham College, Oxford, to provide exhibitions for the Manchester Grammar School boys. Finally, on Walker's retirement as High Master scholars, former scholars and citizens of Manchester subscribed enough money to provide two scholarships of £20 each to be tenable in the school for one year by boys going into the sixth form.

The High Master's passion for external and internal examinations continued unabated. The moment the Civil Service opened its ranks to competition, Walker set about entering his boys. The chairman of the feoffees wrote to Mr Bailey, MP, in 1869 asking him to use his good offices to gain permission for the Manchester Grammar School boys to compete for clerkships in Government offices. In the same year Walker set up a Civil Sevice form in the school.

Walker was also continuing to push through his reform of the school curriculum. Alongside Latin and Greek the boys were accustomed to fairly perfunctory classes in English, French and mathematics. The scheme drawn up for the school by the Court of Chancery in 1848 had added the teaching of science to that of modern languages. Oxford, too, had recognised physics as an academic subject in 1850. Despite this, the Manchester Grammar School had still been unable to afford a physics department when Walker took over as High Master.

For his own part the High Master was perfectly willing to admit that science subjects bored him. They were also very expensive, as he frequently pointed out, once adding 'I believe in Latin grammar and the cane. They are cheap and efficient.' Yet under him at the Grammar School physics and chemistry flourished. From Manchester's new Mechanics' Institute he now recruited as science masters first of all Dr Marshall Watts and then Mr John Angell, poaching two others from Owens College, which a Manchester merchant had recently founded to enable students to follow a university education freed from the religious tests that excluded Nonconformists. John Angell was an inspired teacher, who would enthuse his boys by drawing attention to their own physical faculties, such as eyesight or breathing and then explaining their scientific basis.

Owens College was one of the few institutions in Britain to follow the German method of teaching students science by allowing them to conduct their own experiments. Marshall Watts and John Angell possibly encouraged this method at the Grammar School, but not until the appointment of Francis Jones to succeed Watts in 1872 was the habit wholeheartedly pursued. Jones had studied both at Edinburgh and Heidelberg universities. He stayed at Manchester for half a century.

Few were surprised when the privy council's Science and Arts Department at South Kensington began holding public examinations in 1861 that F. W.

Walker's boys were among the first to take advantage of them. At Speech Day, 1874 he happily announced that pupils from the school had been awarded some 960 certificates and 320 prizes by the department. He had already been able to announce that of the eighteen Natural Science scholarships offered by Oxford University between 1869 and 1871, six had been won by members of the Grammar School's new science sixth.

As for mathematics, when the Schools Enquiry Commission suggested that it should be taught to every boy, Walker asked a Cambridge second wrangler and an Oxford mathematician from Magdalen to draw up for him a new curriculum. The consequence was the creation of a mathematical and physics sixth form, whose boys were entered both for the Oxford local examinations and for the examinations of the Science and Arts Department.

The increasing success of the school brought its rewards. When Walker needed a new mathematics master in 1872, for instance, he received no fewer than 270 applications. The successful applicant stayed at the Manchester Grammar School until 1900.

All this was reinforced outside the classrooms by numerous societies: a biology society, the natural history society and even a steam-engine society which met on Saturday mornings under the guidance of a mathematics master. The boys were inspired to set up societies of their own accord. In 1869 sixteen of them asked Walker's permission to use a classroom once a week to discuss 'Natural Philosophy', and thus the philosophical society came into existence, devoting itself to such burning topics as the Origin of Species, the habitability of the moon, man's relation to nature, and the conflicts between science and religion.

The teaching of art was not neglected, for in 1859 Walker had recruited a talented master named Evans from the Manchester School of Design. Initially the man taught only three hours a week, his salary paid in part by Walker and the usher. Soon the subject was so popular that the feoffees agreed to pay Evans to teach for longer periods in the school, and in 1869 when John Ruskin visited Manchester some of his friends among the feoffees induced him to lecture to the school.

Walker's conviction that the falling off in the number of boys when his reforms first stunned parents would soon cease was abundantly proved correct. As early as 1862 his achievements were attracting more applicants than the school could accommodate. His passionate commitment to examinations led him inevitably to institute the first ever entrance examination to the Manchester Grammar School, to predictable local outrage.

The High Master persisted undeterred, examining the candidates in dictation, English grammar and arithmetic. In 1865 he was turning away as many boys as he accepted, chiefly as he put it 'from want of room and from want of funds.' Walker was adamant, as were the feoffees and his own university examiners, that until the Manchester Grammar School could afford to employ additional masters, 250 boys was the maximum size for his school. As the school's financial problems eased, more boys were admitted. By 1873 the school housed more than 500 boys, by 1874 seventy more, by 1875 a remarkable 700 and by 1876 another fifty. Progress up the school was achieved by success in further periodic examinations, with those boys who did well in the classics having the best chance of rising rapidly.

To house these boys properly was an urgent problem. The school consisted of two distinct buildings some fifty or sixty yards apart. As James Bryce observed in the mid-1860s, neither building had any pretensions to elegance. The schoolrooms in the main building were for the most part quite large enough for the boys they accommodated, as well as being well furnished and ventilated, though Walker would have liked double the space for his classical sixth. The chief defect was that the building covered only a small plot of ground and was thus inconveniently high, with most of the rooms upstairs, approached by a long flight of stone steps and in some cases two flights. 'Thus a good deal of fatigue is caused to the masters and boys, as well as a good deal of noise,' Bryce commented, adding that the High Master 'must also find a greater difficulty in supervising the school generally than he would find if classes were all of them accommodated, as is the case in most schools, upon the ground floor and the first floor only.' That the High Master had also to pass along the street to visit the other building was, in Bryce's opinion, still less desirable. As for the rooms in this second building, which was approached from a small, sunken court, Bryce condemned them as 'not very commodious' and in one case as 'inconveniently dark'.

Long Millgate also stank, for the River Irk had become one of Manchester's open sewers. Since the local authority had demolished the river's weirs, the Irk now frequently flooded the houses of the street and the school itself.

In addition, as James Bryce reported, Long Millgate was 'a mean street, fronting to and bounded on either side by mean houses, some of them shops, others taverns; one, if I remember right, the warehouse of a second-rate undertaker.' He told the Schools Enquiry Commission that drunken men could occasionally be seen staggering past the school door. Yet since the school had no playground, outside the time devoted to lessons the boys had no option but to play in this unsavoury street. Bryce suggested that since Chetham's Hospital seemed to have ample playing space, some of its playground might be ceded to the Grammar School. The governors of Chetham's Hospital refused to help.

Walker himself clearly cared about the physical condition of his boys. He claimed that parents perpetually complained that their sons stooped and were weak in the chest because they lacked the opportunity for proper exercise. He had managed to find a cricket pitch for their use, and in 1868 appointed the school's first gym master. He longed for a gymnasium. Walker continually returned to the need for this gymnasium. 'The desirableness, he should say the necessity, for growing lads, of bodily exercise was too obvious to need comment,' he remarked at Speech Day in 1874, and he declared that he 'often wondered that parents did not insist, even at some personal sacrifice, that adequate provision should be made for what all knew to be an indispendable condition of health.' At the same time he warned of the difficulties: the incredible price of land in the neighbourhood of the school, and the need to provide for such a large number of boys. Nevertheless Walker ventured to predict that before they met again in the Free Trade Hall for another Speech Day, the foundations of the gymnasium would be laid.

Three years later the gymnasium was still to be built, but in his speech on retiring as High Master, Walker had the pleasure of announcing that the governors of the school had definitely adopted a plan to create a spacious gymnasium, library and lecture hall – as he put it, 'a fitting sequel of their past generosity'.

Twelve years earlier, against the disadvantages he had noted, Bryce had set the admirably central position of the school. 'It is close to the Victoria terminus, where the railways from Wigan, Leigh, Bolton, Bury, Rochdale, Oldham, and Ashton converge; it is only half a mile from the London Road station, where the trains from Stockport, and the whole populous district to the south and south west of Manchester enter the city; it is not five minutes walk from Exchange, from which omnibuses run to the most distant suburbs,' he explained. 'This accessibility is an advantage too great to be lost.' In his opinion it was better, therefore, instead of moving the school to an improved neighbourhood, to buy a site for a gymnasium and if possible to obtain land to provide a tolerable playground.

In 1868 it was suggested that the school should move from the centre of Manchester as far away as the suburb of Ladybarn, Fallowfield. The proposal might have ruined the school, for its prosperity and size (and Walker aimed for 1,000 boys) now depended upon the proximity of the railways to bring the pupils from up to thirty miles away into the centre of the now huge and sprawling industrial town.

The solution was to erect new buildings. For the most part the necessary cash was given not by the general public but by the feoffees themselves, in particular the extremely generous Edward R. Langworthy, the Salford alderman who had endowed Peel Park and Peel Public Library. In 1868 he bought a new site in Long Millgate for £1,000 and gave it to the school, along with a further £4,000 towards the cost of a new building. The rest of the feoffees added another £3,600. The parlous economic state of Manchester trade meant that a public appeal was unlikely to prove successful, so Langworthy contributed a further £5,000. Small wonder that on Langworthy's death Walker described him the second founder of the school.

'The scheme under which the school had been allowed freely to adapt itself to the needs of the community,' said Walker, 'had been originated and promoted by Langworthy in concert with two or three of his colleagues, and it was principally to Langworthy himself that they owed their present large and commodious school.' Not until May 1870 was a public meeting held to solicit gifts for the building fund. A year later the school took over its new buildings. They had cost £28,000.

In the meantime every conceivable space was utilised for Walker's growing

*Harry Adnitt's drawing of the door to the 1870 school: imposing Victorian Gothic at the service of education.*

band of boys and masters. Buildings on the corner of Corporation and Cannon Streets had been rented for £100, as well as every free room in Long Millgate. Classics and mathematics were taught in the same crowded rooms. In 1871 the school breathed more easily. At last the mathematics students and the classical boys had rooms of their own. Mr Angell took over part of the former English School. Zachariah Pritchard, arts master since 1869, was given space to teach

65

*A photograph of Long Millgate taken in 1875. The 1870 school building lies on the corner next to the partly hidden gateway to Chetham's.*

his subject throughout the whole school. And the old building of 1776 was now turned into a chemical laboratory for Dr Marshall Watts (who was soon to be dismissed as one of those masters who had refused to teach during the lunch break).

Money still remained an ever-pressing problem, though from the coming of F. W. Walker to Manchester the feoffees had been determined to overthrow the injurious decree of 1849. Hugh Oldham's endowments, which currently were bringing in an income of £2,500 annually, meant that not only the High

Master but also his colleagues were seriously underpaid. Walker at this time was earning an annual salary of £585 and had his house provided. The lowest master was paid a meagre £100 a year, and as Walker observed, 'it is next to impossible to get a man for that money who is fit for the post.' Lack of money was in fact seriously affecting the quality of teachers being attracted to the school. When Walker was in his sixth year as High Master James Bryce declared that some of the teaching at the Manchester Grammar School, particularly that in the sixth form, was remarkably good; but he also found that in some of the lower classes there were faults both in the teaching and the discipline which led him to conclude that the problems of attracting good masters to accept low salaries had a bad effect upon the school. In his view no teacher should be paid less than £200 a year and most should have an annual salary of over £300.

For a time Walker's ambitious plans to treble the size of the school were of necessity shelved; instead the number of boys had to be reduced from 300 to 250. The High Master himself longed for more funds not only to increase the size of the school but also to develop his curriculum. With more money 'we should be able to give a more general system of education', he explained in 1865. 'We should be able to teach physical science, a very expensive matter to teach; we should be enabled to teach German, which is a matter of considerable importance in Manchester, from its great business connexion.'

In 1862 five of the feoffees, with the assistance of the High Master, had been asked to report to the rest 'on the desirability or otherwise of an application being made to the Charity Commissioners in order to obtain their sanction to the establishment of a capitation fee to be hereafter paid by the boys attending the School.' A year later it was decided to ask the Commissioners' permission to charge each boy, apart from fifty free scholars, the sum of £1. 1s a quarter.

Led by an accountant named S. E. Cottam the Old Mancunians rose up in anger against the proposal. The Old Boys' Anniversary Dinner had been founded in 1781 by thirty-two old boys under the leadership of Sir Thomas Egerton, Bart. The members had resolved to elect two stewards and to dine together annually. These annual meetings would welcome masters, and it was hoped that the schoolboys could be given a day's holiday when the Old Mancunians met.

They ate their first dinner together the following year, toasting:

1. Success to the meeting;
2. Success to the School;
3. Success to the Town and Trade of Manchester;
4. The health of Mr Lawson and Mr Darby, who were present as guests.

The successors of these men were devoted to the memory of Jeremiah Smith and Nicholas Germon and implacably opposed to any change in the school they remembered. So great was the animosity of many old boys towards the regime of Frederick William Walker that during his time as High Master the dinners were deliberately discontinued, to be resumed only when he left.

Failing to dissuade the feoffees from going ahead with their attempt to introduce fee payers into the school, the leaders of these old boys petitioned the Charity Commissioners themselves, strongly objecting to the scheme on the grounds that not only poor parents but even the professional classes and tradesmen would find the proposed fee unbearable. At a public meeting in the Town Hall the feoffees found themselves an execrated minority. They were also distressed to learn that Walker was hoping to leave Manchester to become headmaster of Charterhouse.

In the event Walker stayed and the opposition to the feoffees' new scheme gradually broke down. As the feoffees argued, the 'great majority of the boys in the Grammar School were, and always had been, the sons of persons in the middle ranks of life, well-to-do tradesmen, upper clerks, clergymen, and lawyers.' They correctly observed that 'This class will not be deterred by a charge of a quarterly guinea.' By November 1865 the Vice-Chancellor had declared himself basically in favour of the foeffees' proposals. 'If the court of 1849 had known of the decline in income they would hardly have sanctioned so extensive a scheme as was adopted,' he judged. The school's insistence on modern studies as well as the classics required money. 'We do not repeat any attempts to introduce boarders,' the Vice-Chancellor decreed, 'but we submit another method, that of capitation fees.' He therefore allowed the foeffees to raise the school's entrance age to eight, and he endorsed Walker's method of selection by examination.

In spite of a change of Government (and hence of Vice-Chancellor) and further objections from Walker's enemies, in 1867 the feoffees' request was granted, with the proviso that any new accommodation for the proposed 150 fee-paying boys must be paid for by public subscription and not out of the school endowments.

Whether or not they were right to oppose it, S. E. Cottam and his allies were perspicacious enough to have spotted what a revolutionary change was being proposed. The judgement of 1867 enabled the Manchester Grammar School to add to its classical side a modern side, teaching science and modern languages to an equally high level as Latin and Greek. Until 1963 parents had to decide on which side, the modern or the classical, their boys were to be educated. Lafontaine's fables and Emile de Bonnechose's long-forgotten *Erckmann Chatrier, un homme du people* appeared on the curriculum alongside Herodotus, Lucretius, Cicero, Demosthenes, Homer and Aristophanes.

The feoffees accepted their obligation to provide 250 foundation scholars with a free education. Their courage almost broke the school financially, for during F. W. Walker's years as High Master only in 1869 did the books balance. The build-up of fee payers in the school was a slow process. Usually the annual deficit averaged between £700 and £1,000. By 1877 the feoffees were obliged to petition the Charity Commissioners, successfully, for an increase in the fees to twelve guineas a year and a reduction of one third in the number of foundation scholars. Asked whether they should charge more, Walker himself said, 'I think we could educate very decently at 12 guineas.'

In the meantime the High Master was tirelessly soliciting bursaries, exhibitions and scholarships for his boys. One wealthy Manchester businessman, Mr C. F. Beyer, was in conflict with his own workmen when Walker approached him. The High Master boldly took a sovereign from his own pocket, held it in front of the businessman's eyes and cried, 'That's what prevents you from seeing the position of the men.' Beyer was so impressed that he bequeathed £10,000 to the school, money which went to the chemistry laboratory. Other Manchester businessmen subscribed towards exhibitions which enabled Grammar School boys to go on to study free of charge at Owens College and London University, as well as at Oxford, Cambridge and elsewhere.

More than to anywhere else Walker wished to send boys to Oxford or Cambridge, and would go to immense pains to get them there. So successful was he in this that, for instance, in 1863 every one of the boys in Walker's classical sixth form gained an open classical scholarship at either Oxford or Cambridge. He used to teach evening classes at Owens College, where he met Edwin Harrison, when he was mending some property. He was the only son of a mill-girl married to a mechanic. Spotting the young man's potential, Walker took him into the Grammar School even though he was nineteen years old. Four years later Harrison gained a place at Balliol, where the master, Benjamin Jowett, declared him 'the best talker I have ever met'. Jowett observed that given one year's health, 'Harrison will make his mark in Europe.' Instead of a year's health, the prodigy developed a brain disease. 'One day he had a cerebral stroke,' recorded the *Manchester Guardian*; 'he rushed to the window for air, fell on the lawn below, and died at once.'

By contrast the first Manchester boy to win an open scholarship at Balliol under Walker's tuition was Joseph Wood who went on to become headmaster of Harrow. Another of Walker's prodigies was less successful. Martin Geldart was the first of Walker's Manchester pupils to win the 'blue riband' of Oxford, the Balliol scholarship. By Geldart's own account he was 'a sickly, timid, nervous, brooding child with a lively fancy and a restless brain,' admittedly 'given to sulks.' The High Master sent him up as a kind of forlorn hope, with the words, 'He may get it, and he may not,' ringing in Geldart's ears.

As one of his contemporaries observed, Geldart never did his powers justice. 'He became fanciful, over-refined, hypercritical, sensitive, distrustful of his own powers.' Walker took onto his staff 'this lonely and restless soul,' who soon offered himself for holy orders. In advance of his time theologically, he refused to acknowledge that the author of the fourth Gospel was St John, and eventually he became a Unitarian minister. Even this stance seems to have been too dogmatic for Geldart, and soon he gave up working for the church. This strangely wayward man was also a failure as a teacher, for two reasons it was said: 'He was not adapted for continuous and monotonous work;' and 'The impish vivacity of North Country boys almost drove him into a nervous fever.'

In spite of such occasional failures, the report of the Schools Enquiry Commission under Lord Taunton triumphantly vindicated Walker's policies. 'In May 1867 there were 39 undergraduates at Oxford and Cambridge, and of

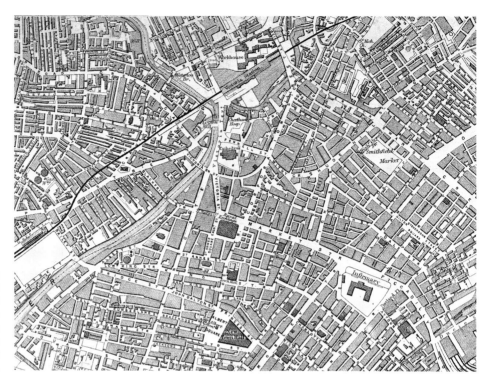

*As boarders were abolished the dawn of the railway age brought boys from the far corners of Lancashire and Cheshire to the school. A map of 1876 shows the school's proximity to Victoria Station. The new 1870 building stands to the right of Chetham's Hospital.*

this the extraordinary proportion of twenty were holding open scholarships or exhibitions' the commissioners observed. 'As much as this cannot be said of any other school in England, and it is all the more remarkable because this School is purely a Day School.' The commissioners went on to assign the credit for this achievement. 'This success must be partly attributed to the ability and exertion of the Head Master, but partly also to the system of admission which fills the School with boys who are best able to profit by the teaching.'

Above all Walker loved his classical sixth form at Manchester. He was ably assisted here by one of Nicholas Germon's former pupils and assistant masters, the Revd George Perkins. Perkins had returned from Brasenose in 1848 to take the post of assistant master in the Lower School. Slowly he rose up the ranks until he finally succeeded Richard Thompson as usher. When Walker decided to resign as High Master, Perkins also said good bye to the school. The two were clearly a well-matched pair, with Perkins diligently backing his High Master's aims and contributing his own skills to teaching the classics.

Walker told the Schools Enquiry Commission in 1865 that with very few exceptions the boys in his class studied the classics exclusively. 'I excuse them even mathematics, unless a boy shows great aptitude for mathematics. If he is a very able boy, I let him pursue both.' Walker added that as mental training for boys of ability under the age of sixteen, his own preference was to teach Greek rather than Latin, and not solely because it was easier to learn. 'I think I see the first dawn of intelligence very often in a boy reading his Xenophon, an intelligence which I do not find when he is reading Caesar,' he confessed.

In consequence Walker saw to it that every form, apart from the very lowest in the school, learned Greek. When a member of the Commission asked him whether he would like to teach Greek and Latin to those who were destined to become small tradesmen and so on, Walker magnificently replied, 'I would teach those languages to peasants, if I had the means and the staff.'

In fact the school catered for very few people who might remotely resemble peasants. As the Taunton Commission noted, although the founder's intention was to offer an education to every social class, 'practically there are very few of the labouring class there.' Instead, as the school returns showed, the school, 'while it has a preponderating number of students from the Middle Class, contains a very important infusion of the Upper Class.' James Bryce had already observed that 'Being a free school, the grammar school is used by all classes of the community,' but he added that the really poor, that is 'those persons who can ill afford to pay *4l. per annum* for their children's schooling', were very scantily represented, constituting less than 6 or 8 per cent of the whole. 'Of the remainder I should conjecture that about one-third are the sons of small shopkeepers, clerks and warehousemen, one-third of the better shopkeepers and merchants of moderate fortune, one-third of professional men,' he noted. 'Owing to its classical character, the grammar school is *par excellence* the school which clergymen, lawyers, and doctors affect for their children.' Bryce added that 'The poor of Manchester, or rather the people who don't wear black coats – the artisans and mechanics, who are often far better off than the clerks – do not think of using the grammar school, because if they desire any education for their children, they desire only reading, writing and arithmetic.'

What Walker did do outside his school was to teach the senior Greek class in the evenings at Owens College. There, he claimed, he had taught young men who started Greek and ended by reading Thucydides. 'I have men in that evening class now who are reading with me the *Apology* of Plato,' he said in 1865. 'They read it slowly, but as intelligently as any undergraduate reads it.'

Walker's own sixth form had no option but to read fast. 'It is needless to say that we worked hard,' one pupil remembered seventy years later. 'I cannot believe that any boy, however self-willed he might be, could have done otherwise under his regime. During my eighteen months in the Sixth, I recollect that we read three or four plays of Aeschylus, two of Aristophanes, the latter twelve books of the Odyssey, and Arrian's Anabasis, as well as some other trifles. In Latin, Virgil, Horace, Ovid, Cicero and Terence were some of the authors that engaged us. We were expected to be prepared with 200 lines of Greek play, and in addition to this some thirty or forty lines of Latin and Greek had to be learnt each day by heart.'

It was during this boy's time that Walker decided to substitute thirty or forty lines of English verse, learnt from Palgrave's *Golden Treasury* for these Latin and Greek poems. 'Of this book I committed about one half to memory,' the old boy recalled, 'and have been for ever grateful for having been made to do so.'

Yet the school was no rigidly narrow hothouse. The creation of a school magazine in 1873 was one means by which Walker inspired a spirit of cohesiveness, camaraderie and endeavour in boys and masters. It offered a translation of the school song, its doggerel verses themselves designed to inspire and encourage the boys (and incidentally inculcating respect for the High Master himself and the ideals he strove for):

*A master shepherds his precious pupils across Long Millgate in Frank Greenwood's turn of the century drawing. On the left stands the 1879 building with the words 'Schola Mancuniensis' over the door. At the far end of the street is the 1880 building inscribed 'Manchester Grammar School'.*

> Hail! ye Owlets, let us joy,
>     While our beaks are callow;
> After our dear youth shall leave us
> Age will come upon us grievous,
>     And soon death will follow.
>
> Honour to our ancient School!
>     Honour to our Master!
> Long may he o'er Owldom rule,
> And wield with glory his ferule,
>     And we learn all the faster.
>
> Honour, too, for every form!
>     Let every Owlet in it,
> Whether classics' prize delight him
> Or Euclid's Elements invite him,
>     Boldly strive to win it.
>
> Let the Owlet, loving Physics,
>     Prizes win and wear them;
> Here let 'Mein Herr,' or 'Monsieur Frog,'
> On, cheek by jowl, to honours jog,
>     And meekly let them bear them.
>
> Let us all with praises crown,
>     Well deserved for ages,
> Hugo, our patron, founder, friend,
> Whose fame and glory ne'er shall end,
>     Who willed us to be sages . . .

To read this first edition of *Ulula* is to be shown a *tranche* of life in a school bounding with activity. M d'Auquier (who had become a devoted follower of Walker, having narrowly avoided dismissal during the furore over lunch-time teaching in 1871) had led a party from smokey Manchester to Paris. One of his boys reported that the Rue du Temple was 'the Deansgate of Paris.' They visited the Tour St Jacques, marvelling at the fact that 4,000 Communards had been buried around it, and in Notre Dame inspected not just the usual treasures but also the blood-stained cassock of Archbishop Darboy, whom the same Communards had recently murdered. The Louvre, the church of St Germain-l'Auxerrois, Vincennes, the Invalides, Montmartre, Versailles (by tramway) and the rest were all duly traversed. The boy who reported for *Ulula* found the interior of the Sainte-Chapelle the most gorgeous he had ever seen: 'there is not an inch which is not covered with painting or gold, and the stained glass is simply glorious.' Three times the boys went to the theatre, and they spent several evenings in *Cafés Chantants*. On the way home they even managed to cram in a visit to Rouen. 'Our readers may thus perceive that idleness is not one of our faults,' the reporter concluded.

Articles on 'the poetical taste of the present day', on 'laughter as a luxury', on the Olympic games and on 'the popular poetry of modern Greece' rubbed shoulders in this first *Ulula* with 'Our Oxford Letter'. This exulted above all in the school's success in taking once again 'the blue riband among university distinctions,' the Balliol scholarship, won for the third time during Walker's stint as High Master by a Manchester Grammar School boy. As well as this gratifying information, the High Master must have read with particular satisfaction the pieces published in this *Ulula* on Greek mythology, on the Greeks and the Persians and on Shakespeare and the classics.

In 1873 the school Debating Society was discussing Wordsworth's fluctuating reputation, slavery, and the abolition of the House of Lords (for, 3; against, 13). The Philosophical Society heard an essay on the economy of the hive bee and another on the circulation of the blood. The Junior Debating Society meditated as to whether Greece had been more beneficial to the world than Rome, whether the Americans were justified in seceding from the mother country, and whether the three manufacturing counties, Lancashire, Yorkshire and Cheshire, 'are the greatest sources of the national prosperity.' Naturally, *Ulula* recorded of the last of these debates, 'the motion met with hardly any opposition, and was unanimously passed.'

After seventeen years in Manchester Walker was offered and accepted the High Mastership, of St Paul's School, London, (having already declined the Corpus professorship of Latin). A lifelong friend of Benjamin Jowett, who had come to a Speech Day in Manchester to praise Walker as England's greatest schoolmaster and the 'one man who had made the School', the High Master went on to transform St Paul's as he had transformed the Manchester Grammar School. After his death in 1910 Walker was justly described as 'a man of great force of character, formidable in opposition alike by his determination and his judgment, but generous and sympathetic as a friend and adviser.' Without such qualities he could not have achieved what he did.

Before he left Manchester all the masters were invited to a delightful and sad farewell dinner. One of them declared that, 'No one who was present will forget the touching speech, in which the great High Master proposed the only toast, nor its fitting conclusion, "from the bottom of my heart I propose, *Floreat Schola Mancuniensis*".' The same master later visited Walker at St Paul's and found him in a poorly-furnished attic, redolent with tobacco smoke. 'His greeting was characteristic. "How do you do? You see we live in squalor here." then, with manifest sincerity, "How is the dear old school?"'

*At the other end of Long Millgate swells and an elegant master ogle street urchins in another Frank Greenwood sketch. By now a stone bridge connects the two wings of the school above Chetham's gateway. This view is similar to that in the photograph on page 66.*

# 5

## Accelerando

### 1877–1903

F. W. WALKER had never met his successor Samuel Dill, but in his retirement speech of 1877 he observed that 'he has been selected for the office of High Master by one of the best and wisest men I have ever known, the President of Corpus, and that is a sufficient warrant for his eminent capacity and fitness.'

Samuel Dill was the last High Master of the Manchester Grammar School to be appointed in this way. The Schools Enquiry Commission had recommended changing the complex and peculiar system by which the Manchester Grammar School was governed. As the Commission described it, the system was indeed peculiar. 'The Feoffees have the general management; but the Dean of Manchester, deriving his power from the extinct office of Warden of the College, is Visitor, and had under the Scheme an indefinite right of supervision of the education: and in conjunction with the Head Master (the Feoffees being umpires) chooses Assistants and Lecturers, and appoints Exhibitioners. Again, the President of Corpus Christi College, Oxford, names the two Foundation Masters, but has no other power; and the Head Master states that in practice he has himself the whole management of the instruction. The Feoffees have a general power of modifying the Regulations.'

*Samuel Dill, High Master 1877–1888, later knighted for his services to education.*

On the Commission's suggestion, the system was changed. Ten years later the powers of the President of Corpus and the Dean of Manchester were abolished, and the feoffees were replaced by governors. Two governors *ex officio* were to be the mayors of Manchester and Salford. The President of Corpus and the Dean of the Cathedral were made governors by courtesy. The rest were either to be co-opted or elected by Oxford and Cambridge universities, and by the local councils, the JPs and the school boards of Manchester and Salford. This was the body that was henceforth to appoint the High Master. The Receiver, given the additional title of clerk to the governors, now was paid a salary of £400 a year.

To follow 'the greatest schoolmaster in England' was no mean task, but Dill was equal to it. Like Walker he was of Irish Protestant stock, born in 1844 the son of the Presbyterian minister of Hillsborough, County Down, and Anna his wife. The Dills were descended from a Dutch soldier who had fought in the army of William III. Again like Walker, Dill was a brilliant Oxford classicist. After taking his first degree at Queen's College, Belfast, he had gone to Oxford, where from Lincoln College he took a first in mods and a first in greats. Corpus elected him a fellow and tutor in 1869.

He came to Manchester just as Walker's dreams of new, commodious school buildings were being realised. On 2 May 1877 The *British Architect and Northern Engineer* announced a public appeal for funds to build this new school. The present buildings, it explained, had been designed for some 600 boys and now were bursting with 800. The old allies of the school had already rallied round. Mr Langworthy's widow had helped by buying yet more land, which could be readily extended by covering the bed of the River Irk. She had also promised further help towards erecting the gymnasium that Walker had long desired, a proposal 'very popular amongst the boys and the assistant masters.' But the feoffees wanted more. The whole project was costed at around £35,000. Mrs Langworthy and Walker's father-in-law Richard Johnson had promised to give £5,000 each. The other feoffees, found £4,350. The gymnasium fund stood at £1,400, and the feoffees were able to promise another £5,000 from the legacy of Mr C. F. Beyer. All the general public needed to contribute was £14,250. So the feoffees appealed to 'the interest and the patriotism of every inhabitant of Manchester and the neighbourhood.'

'The building which it is proposed to erect will contain a very spacious gymnasium, 110ft by 105ft,' the magazine announced. In addition the school proposed to build 'a new and more suitable laboratory; a lecture theatre, large enough to hold several classes at once; a library, boardroom, High Master's room, and necessary offices, with classrooms for 300 scholars.' It was even thought that the outer wall might be adapted to incorporate fives-courts.

By the following July the estimated cost of the building had risen to £40,000, but of this £31,000 had already been raised. More details of the plans, designed by the firm of Mills and Murgatroyd, were now available. A three-storey building was proposed, incorporating also a basement, half of which would be given over to the gymnasium, the other half comprising smaller rooms and a dining hall, 130ft by 35ft. The first floor of the building would house the lecture theatre and nine classrooms; the next floor, the 'chemical school', comprised a laboratory and study rooms; and the top storey was to be given over to rooms for recreation, reading and preparatory school work.

By October 1880 the building was finished, lauded by the *British Architect* as 'one of the most completely finished buildings of its kind in the kingdom, and having a gymnasium, considered by authorities in such matters, second to none in Europe.' Thirty feet high, its projected dimensions had expanded to 120ft by 135ft. Its floor consisted of a layer of sawdust six inches thick, on top of which was packed a foot of hair covered with a huge single canvas sheet. Five hundred boys at once could now drill indoors *en masse*. They had the use of one hundred pairs of dumb-bells, one hundred bar-bells, ladders, parallel and horizontal bars, horses and a large dressing room.

*The gymnasium finally in use. A photograph from before the First World War, showing John MacAuley who drilled boys from 1898–1945.*

*Basket ball practice in the gym today.*

Exploiting these new opportunities for physical exercise, the boys, as a *Ulula* correspondent wonderingly observed, were developing impressively muscular chests, with the lower boys putting on an average extra inch and the higher boys around one-and-a-half inches. In addition the new gymnasium soon acquired a less happy aspect, for miscreants among the boys could be punished by extra half hours of drill. The gym, the same correspondent noted, now and then became a kind of purgatory where heinous offences were tediously expiated.

The school had been more than doubled in extent. It now boasted a commanding frontage, and as the current volume of *Ulula* recorded, its internal appearance had been quite changed, 'making light and cheerful that which was formerly thought somewhat prison-like and unattractive.' This did not mean that the outside environment had been improved. The school was well aware of its deficiencies and constantly vigilant to remedy them. The Receiver's report for 1878 noted the 'settlement of questions of light and air over the proposed new buildings of Chetham's Hospital and [the brewers] Boddington, Leith, Buss and Higgin.' As late as 1895 the Royal Commission on Secondary Education was lamenting that, 'The street (Mill Lane) into which the school opens is still a row of mean shops with all their undesirable surroundings.' The boys seem not to have minded. One of their favourite school songs went so far as to compare the Manchester Grammar School to one of the surrounding factories. At Speech Days the children of the owl proudly bellowed:

> Round us are factory, forge and store,
>   Market and cattle-pen;
> But here in our factory, 'mid the roar
>   Work we at making men. . .
>   Tuwhit, tuwhoo,
>   Be brave, be true,
>   Tuwhit, tuwhoo, tuwhoo,
> Minerva's son art thou.

In December 1880 Dill was delighted to host a public reception in the new school building. A year later the exercise was repeated, but on a much more impressive scale. The new building was crammed with boys' activities, the Debating Society in charge of everything, twenty young gymnasts going through their newly developed paces, the Philosophical Society performing scientific experiments, the Natural History Society and the school's art department laying on exhibitions.

The plethora of extra-curricular activities continued to expand. Swimming contests began in 1881. A cricket field was rented, and a Rifle Corps established. In September 1882 the masters played the boys at cricket, with the astonishing result that the masters' eleven made 18 runs in its first innings, the boys countered with a score of 145, and the masters were all out in their second innings for a miserable 25. Athletics involved leaping over poles, a stone race and a sack race, and culminated in a magnificent annual sports day. A rugby football club was established, and in 1881, with even-handed respect to the two ancient English universities, adopted as its sportswear an Oxford blue cap, white knickerbockers and a Cambridge blue jersey. Even so, the club had difficulty enlisting enough members, and *Ulula* was soon complaining that in some cases only eight or nine men were turning up to play, with the consequence that 'every match has been a fiasco.'

Theatre was now becaming a regular feature of school life – or at least the performance of truncated plays. In 1881 and 1882 the boys were treated to scenes from Aristophanes's *Knights*, to part of Goldsmith's *She Stoops to Conquer* and to a production of sections of Molière's *Le Médecin malgré lui*. In the Glee Club boys and masters not only sang together; they also enjoyed pianoforte and violin solos. Concert goers relished M. d'Auquier's sterling performances of Poniatowski's *The Yeoman's Wedding*. No longer wandering aimlessly in dank Long Millgate, other boys were occupying their spare time in playing chess or draughts.

Along with his new building Dill had also inherited a changed pattern of free and paying boys. On 30 April 1877 a scheme under the Endowed Schools Acts became law reducing the number of free boys from 250 to 153 (a direct imitation of the pattern at St Paul's School and a number apparently adopted from the miraculous draught of fishes caught by St Peter). These free places were now to be filled by competition among boys at elementary schools. By 1883 the school was educating 949 boys, 796 of them paying fees.

Though an exceedingly distinguished classicist, Dill instantly perceived the need to develop still further the modern side of his school. 'You will soon have in Manchester what has long been regarded as unattainable,' he promised in 1886: 'a modern education which shall be at once thorough as a discipline and complete as a preparation for commercial life.' French, German, history, English literature and philology, mathematics and physics were the basic components of this course. The former English school of 1835 was transformed into a physics laboratory, to complement the laboratory in the new building (which was named after its generous benefactor Mr Beyer). By 1888 the modern side consisted of 411 boys, compared with only 279 in 1879, and Dill had created a Modern Sixth form in the place of the old Civil Service form. The results of his policy were gratifying at the highest academic level. In 1885–86, for example, the school gained eighteen university scholarships and exhibitions, six of them in classics, seven in science, three in mathematics and one in modern history.

Dill was acutely aware that many able boys from the elementary schools were still being withdrawn far too early by their parents and sent out to work, even though their education was provided entirely free of charge. He accordingly suggested that the feoffees should offer such boys annual maintenance grants of twelve guineas, in an attempt to persuade them to stay on at school.

*Harry Adnitt's drawing of the dour library in the 1880 building, home of the classical sixth.*

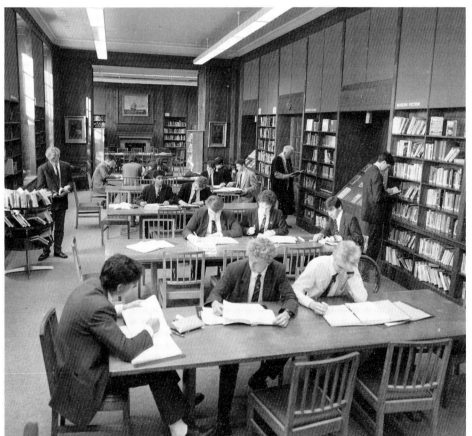

*The Paton Library, 1989.*

A further alleviation of this perennial problem was at hand in the new practice of the Manchester School Board of giving able scholars exhibitions substantial enough to maintain them at secondary schools, a plan devised to increase the number of recruits into the teaching profession. Walker's energetic fostering of university scholarships was emulated by his successor, and soon Dill was able to announce that the number of scholarships tenable either at the school or at university had risen to fifty-four.

These privileged boys and dedicated masters of the Manchester Grammar School were not without social consciences. In the late 1880s a working lads' club had been founded by a Mr Alexander Devine in Ancoats. It soon ran into financial trouble, and Devine had the idea of appealing for help to the boys of the Manchester Grammar School. Governors, pupils, old boys and Dill himself responded with alacrity. At a meeting held in the lecture theatre in January 1888 Dill's proposal that a club for working lads living in the Oldham Road/Rochdale Road area be established with the support of Old Mancunians and friends of the school, was enthusiastically accepted. Premises were soon found in Livesey Street, and on 20 October the Duke of Clarence officially opened the Hugh Oldham Lads' Club.

By then Dill had resigned as High Master to pursue his academic studies. By 1890 he was Professor of Greek at Queen's College, Belfast. A stream of noted books on ancient history poured from his pen. He never lost interest in the education of the young, chairing the vice-regal committe of enquiry into primary education in 1913 and 1914, as well as the Intermediate Board of Education for Ireland. In 1909 his services to education were rewarded with a knighthood.

Dill had been a fine teacher and an impressive High Master. After his death the President of Corpus, Sir Richard Livingstone, quoted the testimony of one of Dill's Manchester pupils, Gordon Hewart (by then Viscount Hewart). Dill, said Hewart, possessed a striking personality, equally magnificent in form and shy and reserved in speech. 'He was', the former pupil testified, 'one of the very few men who appear to the boy to be heroes, and throughout life never lose that character.'

Yet the valedictory words of this distinguished academic to the Manchester Grammar School had stressed Dill's ambition not so much for its intellectual fruitfulness as for the success of its corporate life, a creative and character-building solidarity which he had endeavoured to foster through music, through athletics, through societies and through literature. 'The position of the School as a competitor in examination is already ensured,' he said. 'Its great weakness, the absence of a common life outside the classroom, is in process of being ended. If you can overcome the difficulties completely, the last reproach against day-school life – that it fails to form the boy's character – will be wiped out, and your Grammar School will stand even higher in its influence and in its distinction than it does today.'

In spite of his largeness of spirit, Samuel Dill's religious views were powerfully, even rigidly Protestant, and even his admirers noted that he became even more entrenched as an Irish Presbyterian in his years at Belfast. By contrast his successor as High Master, Michael George Glazebrook, had a far more flexible religious outlook, entering enthusiastically, intelligently and committedly into the religious controversies of his day.

Two years after coming to Manchester he was ordained an Anglican priest in Manchester Cathedral. In opposition to the Catholic movement in the Church of England as well as to traditional Roman Catholicism, Glazebrook had little time for outward show in religion, maintaining that 'large numbers of Churchmen are in open revolt against the authority of the Bishops – and why? Because they would substitute the material for the spiritual – incense for a prayer, a material miracle for a spiritual power, a verbal confession to a priest for the opening of the heart to God.' He eschewed dogmatism and embraced modernism to such an extent that his *Faith of a Modern Churchman*, published in 1918, was to attract the wrath of Frederick Henry Chase, the learned but traditionalist Bishop of Ely. Glazebrook was equally learned, as his *Commentary on the Apocalypse*, published five years later, revealed.

These religious views apart, Glazebrook came to Manchester with impeccable educational credentials. Though he was born in London, his was an old Lancashire family. After a spell at Brentford Grammar School as a boy he had entered Dulwich College and become head of the school. In 1872 he went up to Balliol as a mathematical scholar, taking a first in the mathemathics and classical moderations, followed by a second in his final mathematics school and a first in *literae humaniores*. At Oxford he combined this intellectual prowess with athletics, representing the university against Cambridge in the hundred yards and high jump (in which he became amateur champion in 1875).

Glazebrook left university for a life of adventure, travelling in particular in Mexico until in 1878 Dr H. Montagu Butler enticed him to Harrow as an assistant master. Ten years later he was High Master of the Manchester Grammar School. He had already edited the plays of Euripides, and his edition of Aeschylus came out in the year of his appointment. His duties as High Master failed to interrupt his stream of publications. In 1891 he published a junior course of *Lessons from the Old Testament* which had gone through six editions by 1902. His senior course on the same subject, also written during his years at Manchester, was equally successful. And in 1891 he and C. E. Vaughan began editing an extremely popular series of English classics for schools.

Glazebrook also greatly sympathised with one of the most recent developments at the Manchester Grammar School, the founding of the Hugh Oldham Lads' Club. At Balliol he had been profoundly influenced by Arnold Toynbee, whose work among the London poor with Canon Barnett, Vicar of St Jude's Whitechapel, had led to the foundation of the first university East End settlement, Toynbee Hall, shortly after Toynbee's death in 1883. Under such influences Glazebrook in Manchester was instantly drawn to the Hugh Oldham Lads' Club, and became chairman of its committee, apparently entrancing the working class youths with his lantern lecture, 'A visit to Norway'.

*Michael George Glazebrook, High Master 1888–1891. This portrait hangs in Clifton College. It is a copy of the contemporary portrait which was destroyed during the Second World War.*

*The art hall as seen by Harry Adnitt at about the turn of century, with a gladiator dying in front of the mighty organ.*

*A photograph of the art hall, taken in the early years of this century. Freddy Garnett, the art master was assisted by two ladies, one of whom, 'Ma Whitworth' is seen here.*

He also set about raising money to level the school's new athletics ground, and in his reign as High Master both a harriers and a hockey club were founded. No doubt his Christian instincts warmed as the boys at Speech Day annually yelled words penned by their High Master:

> 'True and tender' be our maxim,
>   Whatsoever chance befall.
> 'True and tender, true and tender,
>   Each for other, God for all.'

But the same jingle also proclaimed:

> Fair and fickle is the southland,
>   True and tender is the North. . .
> Theirs the glow of golden harvests,
>   Laughter of the sunlit sea;
> Ours the grey of barren mountains,
>   And the wild wind blowing free. . .
> Theirs the green of softer meadows,
>   Rippling of pellucid rills;
> Ours the din of dusty highways,
>   And the frowning fronts of mills.
> Theirs a calm pervading beauty
>   Flowering at the cotter's door;
> Ours a sterner beauty banished,
>   Lingering by the lonely moor. . .
> Theirs the charm of courtly graces,
>   Softer speech and gentler ways;
> Ours the strength of self-reliance
>   And the candour that we praise.

The fair and fickle southland, the green of softer meadows, the charm of courtly graces were irresistibly beckoning Michael George Glazebrook himself. Within two years of coming to Manchester he was gone, to take up the post of headmaster of Clifton College.

Yet in his short time at the school he had made some major changes. Despite Samuel Dill's energetic attempts to strengthen the modern side of the school, boys weak in classics were still at a disadvantage in winning scholarships. Glazebrook persuaded the governors to give more importance to mathematics, modern languages and English literature in choosing which boys were to be offered financial support at the school. He also tightened the academic screw on boys still further by instituting fortnightly reports, to be taken home by each pupil and signed by his parents.

Glazebrook knew how to delegate. For the first time form masters were allowed to make contact with parents. In thus taking more responsibility for their boys, the form masters counteracted to some extent the dread caused by fortnightly reports. Hitherto a boy's homework could easily have been set quite independently by four or even five masters, none of them paying any regard to how much the pupil was being burdened by the other members of the staff. Form masters now began to take general responsibility for the burden of work assigned to each pupil. In a similar reform, one master was put in overall charge of modern languages.

Frederick William Walker's insistence that he had but one school had not prevented his insistence that the sixth form was the *crème de la crème*, even to the extent of allowing sixth formers to have prayers in their own rooms separate from the rest of the school. Glazebrook corrected this anomaly. The beneficial effect of sixth form boys mingling with the rest of the school was enhanced when he appointed some of the higher boys as prefects to take responsibilities in controlling and disciplining their younger contemporaries.

These reforms apart, in his short-lived term as High Master Glazebrook enthusiastically developed what he had inherited. When the school was bequeathed £2,000 in 1889, Glazebrook divided the spoils into reading prizes, prizes for the modern side of the school, money for the purchase of a school organ and for establishing a workshop, setting the rest aside to equip adequately the physics laboratory he had inherited from the regime of Samuel Dill. Glazebrook, for all his emphasis on the modern side of his school, did not despise the superb classical foundation on which the reputation of the Manchester Grammar School had been built, even though times were changing.

The last Speech Day at Manchester over which he presided was graced by the headmaster he had served at Harrow, now Master of Trinity College Cambridge and Vice-Chancellor of the University. As well as presenting the prizes, Dr Butler addressed the boys on the need to preserve Greek and Roman thoughts in school life – 'by means of English translations'.

M. G. Glazebrook's devotion to the Christian religion led him to intersperse it even into the classical sixth. But his educational creed was equally inspired by English literature. As he himself put it, passionately and romantically, in 1889:

> Let our boys live as much as may be in the presence and in the contemplation of the strong, the beautiful, the noble, who look out upon them from the pages of Scott and Spenser and Shakespeare. Let them try to picture such characters, in order that they may imitate them. Let them learn by heart the utterances of heroes, that their tongues may be attuned to heroic strains. And when their blood is fired by scenes of noble action or suffering, and their hearts touched by noble sentiment, they will unconsciously absorb a noble style.

Glazebrook stayed at Manchester for so short a time that the achievements of the school under his regime inevitably reflected on his predecessor and staff. These achievements continued to be prodigious. For example, the impressive list of honours printed in the Speech Day programme for 1889 laconically included under the item Miscellaneous Successes 'Fletcher L., M.A. . . . Fellow of the Royal Society'.

Glazebrook's successor, John Edward King, continued to build on these foundations. King started work in January 1891. Educated at Clifton, at the time of his call to Manchester he had been a fellow of Lincoln College, Oxford, for nearly ten years and had also taught under Walker at St Paul's. In the early years of his tenure of office at Manchester art blossomed at the school, and by 1892 the boys were modelling in clay. Drama flourished still

*J. E. King, High Master 1891–1903, upholding the standards of the school.*

more, and in December 1891 no less a genius than Sir Henry Irving was visiting the school to encourage the boys and offer some impromptu coaching.

Music probably outstripped both art and drama. In Mr George Broadfield the school was blessed with a music fanatic who was also a teacher of genius. Both as conductor and accompanist he had fostered the twenty-year-old Glee Club for the past ten years of its life. In 1890 he conducted and accompanied a rousing performance of *The Ancient Mariner*. *Iolanthe* and *Pinafore* became standard items in the Glee Club repertoire. In May 1894 the Club felt competent enough to tackle successfully the first part of Mendelssohn's *Elijah*, save for the chorus 'The fire descends'. Broadfield himself sang the aria 'Is not His word like a fire?' The following Christmas the Club's *pièce de résistance* was 'The Earl King's Daughter', when, as a spectator noticed, 'some of the audience showed their appreciation, as is customary at Sir Charles Hallé's and other concerts in Manchester, by leaving early.'

In the same year an Orchestral Society was founded. Sterndale Bennett's *May Queen*, performed with choir and orchestra in 1897, won rapturous applause. Soon the orchestra was attempting such works as the overture to *The Merry Wives of Windsor* and selections from Haydn's Eleventh Symphony. And gifted boys now began to win music scholarships at the universities, as well as scholarships to the newly-founded Royal Manchester College of Music. George Broadfield continued to serve the Manchester Grammar School until 1902, when he retired, a silver-bearded patriarch whose eyes still gleamed with enthusiasm.

As for sport, King's era saw the purchase of the playing fields which till then had merely been rented. Initially the school hoped, with the enthusiastic help of old boys led by Sir William H. Bailey, to buy two separate playing fields, one in north Manchester, the other on the south side of the city, but funds ran out and only the north site was bought. Mr Murgatroyd, architect, was then commissioned to build a pavilion at the cost of £1,125. The inaugural match was played in the presence of several ladies, including the Lady Mayoress who hoisted and unfurled a flag. The presence of these women apparently quite unnerved the cricketers, unused to 'the fire of ladies' eyes'.

The shadow of war, presaging a yet greater trauma, fell over the school towards the end of King's career at Manchester. In 1899 an open meeting had been held to test the feeling of the school with regard to forming a Cadet Corps. Enthusiasm for the project was sufficient for an approach to be made to seek permission of the governors for such a venture. Before that year was out the second Boer War had begun, and old boys were faced with real and not make-believe manoeuvres. They acquitted themselves with honour in the conflict, and an Old Mancunian, Lieutenant W. H. S. Nickerson of the Royal Army Medical Corps, was one of the first British officers to win the Victoria Cross for bravery against the Boers.

Judged purely on its academic successes, the Manchester Grammar School under King remained pre-eminent in the land. By now it was divided into three sides: classical, modern and special – the last divided into three

*George Broadfield: genius, musician, fanatic.*

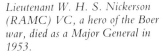

*Lieutenant W. H. S. Nickerson (RAMC) VC, a hero of the Boer war, died as a Major General in 1953.*

departments concentrating on mathematics specialists, science specialists and boys hoping to matriculate at London or Victoria (Manchester) universities. At all levels, the success of its pupils was rarely matched by the pupils of rival schools. As the brilliant Manchester scientist Sir Lazarus Fletcher (a former pupil of F. W. Walker) pointed out at the Old Mancunians dinner in 1896, in the past twenty-four years ninety-two open science scholarships and exhibitions at Oxford and Cambridge had been won by Manchester Grammar School boys. Forty-four of these boys had taken first class degrees, and fifteen second class. The Grammar School scarcely needed to blow its own trumpet. In 1895 a member of the Royal Commission on Secondary Education reported that 'The Manchester Grammar School in every way stands far ahead of any other Secondary School in my district; the advanced character of the education given, the largeness of the area from which it draws its day boys, and the extraordinary number of boys which it sends up annually to the universities, not only distinguish it from other Lancashire schools, but give it a foremost and in some respect the foremost place among the great day schools of England.'

The Commissioner who wrote this, F. E. Kitchener, was equally impressed by the distances boys were prepared to travel to reach the school. 'When I went in the hundred of Salford, and, indeed, in most parts of West Derby, I did not fail to recognise by their school caps the Manchester Grammar School boys on their way by rail to and from the school.' More than thirty boys attended from places over twenty miles from Manchester. These included two boys from Todmorden, 21 miles away, thirteen from Blackburn, 24 miles away, six from Burnley, 25 miles away, and three from Southport, 37 miles away. A sixth of the school lived over ten miles from Manchester and two-thirds outside the city limits. The Royal Commission was impressed enough to stick in its report copies of a map prepared by the High Master plotting the homes of his boys.

Kitchener did not truly approve of all this, for – apart from the cost of travel and the wear and tear on the travellers – to him it revealed the paucity of good education elsewhere in the great Manchester conurbation. In Manchester itself this lack was already being remedied by the new School Board set up by the 1870 Education Act and financed by rates levied by the city council. In 1881 the Ducie Avenue Board School was opened as a higher grade school, and three years later Peter Street School and Lower Moseley Street School combined to form a new central school in Deansgate. Soon Manchester possessed six higher grade schools, with bursaries of £7 to £13 available to enable poorer boys from the elementary schools to continue their secondary education. These establishments began to compete with the Grammar School for the brighter boys of Manchester, and in 1885 for the first time Samuel Dill noticed a decline in the number and quality of elementary schoolboys competing for his scholarships. The foundation of Hulme Grammar School in Alexandra Park, followed by resuscitation of the William Hulme school in Oldham, cut a further swathe into the number of able boys applying for places

*Opposite: The map, included in the 1895 Royal Commission on Secondary Education Report, which shows the exceptionally wide catchment area from which the school drew its pupils. On the original map, Grammar School boys were marked by red dots. Here these show as grey (as opposed to the black railway stations). An interesting comparison can be made with the map showing the homes of today's Manchester Grammar School boys, on page 133.*

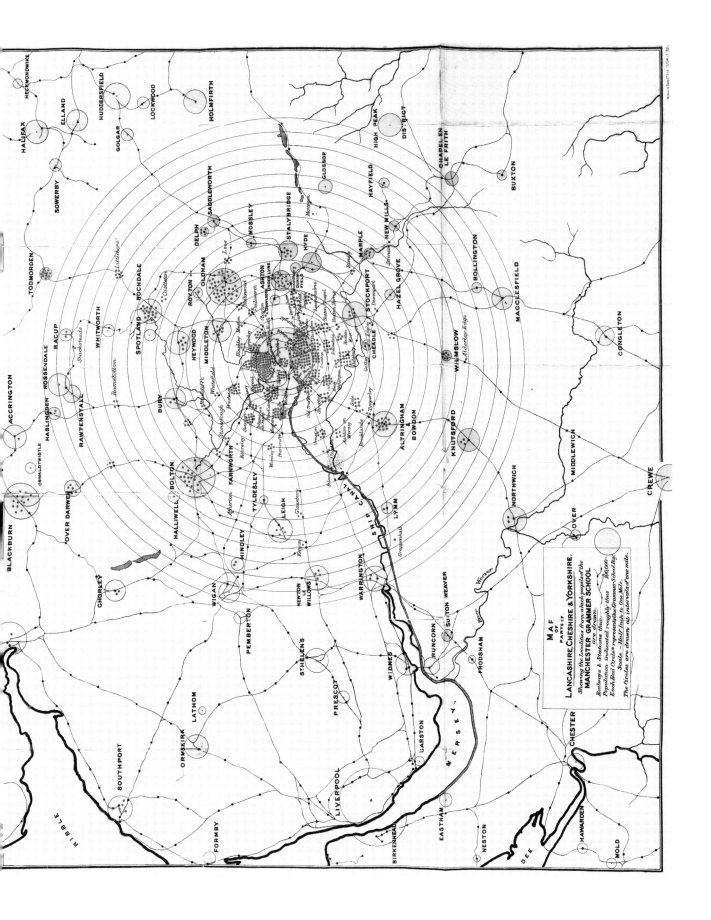

at the Manchester Grammar School. The school roll began to fall: 815 in 1887; 781 in 1889; 761 in 1890. As the roll fell, Dill's successor had kept his nerve. In 1890, rather than accept less able boys, Glazebrook had deliberately rejected thirty applicants, a decision 'necessary in the best interests of the school.'

Three feeder preparatory schools, set up in North Manchester, South Manchester and Sale, helped to alleviate the problem, and the school roll of the Manchester Grammar School stabilised itself at around 800 pupils. The 1902 Education Act and its subsequent modifications made life easier, for now local authorities were empowered to offer scholarships and bursaries to pupils passing from their elementary schools to such endowed schools as Manchester. More and more able children got a foot on the educational ladder.

A year later John Edward King resigned, to become headmaster of Bedford Grammar School. His former colleagues gave the departing High Master and Mrs King a goblet-shaped silver flower vase, ornamented round the rim with figures from the Elgin marbles. The boys gave them a handsome silver centre-piece for their table. King's parting address at the Old Mancunians' dinner in April emphasised the strengths as he saw them of the school he had led for nearly thirteen years: its openness to any boy of ability; its adaptability to the needs of a scientific age, while maintaining its long-cherished traditions; and its dedication to good manners and good learning.

King's educational philosophy had been to provide what was popularly known as 'a ladder of education,' an essential ingredient, he maintained, in a genuinely democratic society. For many the Manchester Grammar School did provide that ladder. Ernest Barker, for instance, joined the school with a foundation scholarship in 1886. He was to end a distinguished career as Principal of King's College, London; Professor of Political Science; and Fellow of Peterhouse, Cambridge. 'Coming from my cottage, I had nothing but my school,' he later acknowledged, 'but having my school, I had everything.'

After King's resignation in 1903 the *Saturday Review* acknowledged his success in building such an educational ladder in Manchester. 'No Secondary School in the country is doing so much to bridge over the gulf between the Board Schools and the University,' the *Review* asserted. 'Its successes are not selfish and individual. They are genuine democratic triumphs, which, if we may be allowed to employ a much abused word in its broader and truer senses, possess social and political, as well as scholastic importance.'

His successor, one of the most renowned schoolmasters of the twentieth century, embodied these democratic instincts in every fibre of his body and intellect.

# 6

## The Maestro

### 1903–1924

'REMEMBER you who are now boys are the makers of the future. You are training for this. Aim high, and make a daily effort towards this. In playing your games see what qualities they bring out. If these are manliness, straightforwardness, promptness, courage, good temper in defeat, kind-heartedness, these are the true equipment for life: – make them yours by quiet, daily effort.' The speaker was G. F. Watts at a speech day. Sitting next to him on the platform was one of the school's greatest High Masters, and he made these words his own. Manliness, straightforwardness, promptness, courage, good temper in defeat and kind-heartedness were the ideals which J. L. Paton strove to inculcate in his boys. He noted the words down as Watts spoke, and would subsequently often quote them as the aims of the 'all round training' – of body, character, in social and intellectual life – which a great school should provide.

King's successor, John Lewis Alexander Paton, or J. L. Paton as he was universally known, fitted effortlessly into that stream of Godly and scholarly men who had run the Manchester Grammar School since the middle of the previous century. But there was also an unusually radical element in his background. J. L. Paton's father, John Brown Paton, was descended from Scottish Covenanters, one of whom had been hanged and another shot. The future High Master always kept a print of the former's execution hanging on the wall of his home. Paton's was a family ready if necessary to rebel.

John Brown Paton, principal of the Congregational Theological College at Nottingham, was a social reformer as well as a far-sighted educationalist. In devoting his life to teaching, his second son, though a remarkable scholar, produced only one major book: a biography of his father. As it describes how his father grappled with the educational questions of the day, the book reveals both the tenor of J. L. Paton's own mind and the deep influence of his Nonconformist home.

The Education Bill of 1902, scarcely twelve years old when Paton was writing, had reopened the floodgates of controversy beween Nonconformists

*The imposing brow and piercing eyes of the great J. L. Paton, High Master from 1903–1924.*

and the established church. John Brown Paton had been one of those dissenters who, along with several enlightened Anglican bishops, had worked out a pattern of worship and religious instruction in state schools that could prevent the rankling discord, bitter feeling and continuous strife engendered by age-long ecclesiastical differences. Some of his words express his son's ambition as a schoolmaster: to 'symbolise the common Christian faith of our land, and to teach it in a way wholly delightful.' This was an ideal to which J. L. Paton clung throughout his long and fruitful life. Unfortunately the Government of the day did not share his father's eirenic nature. The act of 1902 promoted strife. On principle Paton's father refused to pay the education rate, and the bailiffs distrained his goods.

J. L. Paton remained a faithful son of John Brown and Jessie Paton, dedicated to his father's belief that the Christian religion, taught by men and women of integrity, produced in children what was in those days known as character, 'the best asset, it has been said, of a nation's wealth,' as John Brown Paton put it, 'the best guarantee of its industrial energy, and the strongest bulwark of its security.'

In quoting his father J. L. Paton set out his own creed as a teacher and High Master. 'The right sort of reading should be encouraged, and good songs, ennobling pictures should be hung on school walls; instruction should be given in the laws of health and Christian conduct; the evils of intemperance, gambling and other vices should be pointed out; by organising and supervising games, teachers could promote manliness, self-control and a love of fair play; the formation of Old Scholars' Associations would help to perpetuate the good influence of the school.' All of these things this extraordinary man brought to the Manchester Grammar School. Education, said John Brown Paton, was essentially a religious matter, given on a religious basis and under religious inspiration. As a true Protestant he held this religion to be based essentially on the Bible. The Bible, he maintained, presented the highest ideal of life, a basis without which the very state would founder. These were ideals from which his son never swerved.

The second of four sons of this Congregational minister whose spiritual mark on Nottingham and indeed the nation was remarkable, Paton – like his brothers – never married. His Manchester home in Broughton Park was run by his sister Mary. He had been educated in Germany at the Halle Gymnasium, at Shrewsbury (where he was head of the school) and at St John's College, Cambridge. There he took firsts in parts I and II of the classical tripos and won the Junior Chancellor's medal. He was immediately elected a fellow of his college and with equal alacrity took up his life's vocation. Experience in teaching at the Leys School, Cambridge, soon brought him the post of lower bench master at Rugby.

Here some of the characteristic interests of Paton were already manifesting themselves. As well as teaching the sons of the privileged and running the sixth form, Paton was organising classes for working men and was frequently in their homes. He was discovered doing the housework of a sick working-class mother. He proudly led his Boys' Life Brigade through the streets of the town. As Paton was fond of asking, 'What does the future clergyman bred at a public school, know of the working classes?' His answer was that, 'Too often the boy learns to despise the great body of his species with a contempt bred not by familiarity but by lack of it.' At least under Paton Rugby boys had their noses rubbed in the earthy life of their less fortunate contemporaries.

When he left Rugby in 1898 to run University College School, London, Paton did not abandon these interests and ideals, for the school had established a Working Boys' Club whose activities Paton enthusiastically espoused. The middle class parents discovered that their boys were painting the playing-field railings. And the fanatical Germanophile that was the new headmaster was imitating the Teutonic *Wandervögel* movement by leading boys on camps and hikes which included open-air bathing, as well as taking them on arduous runs over Primrose Hill.

Paton's father, his son wrote, saw how the growing organisation of industrial life enormously increased the moral dangers both for boys and girls. Play, music and colour, song, art and rhythmic movement could entice a child away from this moral danger. 'He saw that in the great public schools the moral tone was fostered by the corporate life, the organised team-games, the personal influence of masters, the continued attachment of scholars after they had left,' wrote J. L. Paton, simultaneously expressing part of his own creed as a teacher. 'These same elements he wished to see in the schools of the poorest.' Startlingly, on being appointed in 1903 to head the finest day school in

*The lure of scouting, another Paton innovation.*

England Paton remarked, 'I am looking forward to being able to do something for poor boys.'

He kept his word. As one old boy recalled, 'He knew which of us came from poor homes, and in such cases he would help unostentatiously, often without our knowledge.' The terminal book and stationery bill would not be presented. The fees for the Northern Universities Matriculation Examination would not be exacted, and so on. He took boys into his own house, and for them and others he paid the expenses of the treks and other enjoyable exercises which would otherwise have been beyond their reach. Part of Paton's quarrel with the public schools was that they provided education only for such as could afford it. At the Manchester Grammar School he strove to realise what he called the true principle on which we must work in future: 'that education is for all as can receive it.'

Writing about the secondary education of the working classes Paton contrasted the son of well-to-do parents at the age of thirteen with a child of the poor. The former is transferred from preparatory to public school, his parents if necessary making strenuous monetary sacrifices in his interest. The working class boy of the same age faces a far different prospect, perhaps already doing a milk or newspaper round before he goes to school in the morning or, if he lives in one of the textile towns, 'being broken in to his future vocation as a "little piecer" at the loom.' The smarter working class boy might end up in an office or as an apprentice to some skilled trade, but the great majority is bundled into whatever job happens to come to hand: 'he runs errands for the local grocer, gets his stand on the tram-route for paper-selling, weighs out soap-powder into cardboard boxes, puts labels on soda-water bottles, packs tea, chops wood, drives a pony down the pit, or surveys the world from the tail-end of a delivery van.' Instead of working from 9 to 4.30 with a generous interval at midday he now turns out at the sound of the 5.30 alarm and has no time to call his own for the next twelve hours.

Yet these adolescent years from thirteen to seventeen, the High Master of the Manchester Grammar School argued, are the most crucial ones in a person's life. 'All the powers of body, mind, and character are then in their most plastic condition. These are the years of preparation for the crises of sex and domestic independence. At no other time of life does external environment and influence, whether good or evil, count for so much as then. At no other time is right training and supervision more important.' The voluntary system of secondary education was in Paton's view no longer adequate to cope with the needs of such boys. National compulsory education was vital. The hours of juvenile labour must be adjusted. Curricula deliberately designed to dovetail with the duties of practical life were called for, and not simply for the exceptionally intelligent adolescent. 'Provision must be made for the dull and coarse who will never rise above the rank of labourer,' Paton insisted, lamenting that, 'The present system offers them nothing.'

Paton turned on the legislators of his age that notion of an educational ladder which had so much inspired his predecessor. 'We have spoken much of "the

*J. L. Paton's sanctum.*

ladder of education",' he observed. 'The phrase has grown a trifle musty, but while we have provided for the few the ladder from the elementary school to the University, we have not yet provided for the many the ladder between the elementary school and those industrial and commercial occupations on which the very existence of our country depends.'

Finally he urged the need for social solidarity. 'In the battle of life, which is based on the principle of each for himself and the devil take the hindmost, we fight each for our own hand, and grow into hardened individuals,' he declared. 'To this tendency the best corrective is to find ourselves members of a society in which the efficiency and good name of the whole depend on the efficiency and honourable conduct of each constituent member.'

These were not the thoughts of an indolent bystander. Paton noted that, 'The biggest evening schools of Manchester are found in connection with the large Working Lads' Clubs of that city, and no development of recent years is so full of promise as this.' Paton of course had his own Hugh Oldham Lads' Club. He adored it. 'In the back streets of the Manchester slums there stands an old disused police station,' he wrote: 'it is now a Boys' Club. Where the police recruits once drilled, their quondam victims now disport themselves on horizontal bars and other gymnastic apparatus; in their cells where prisoners slept off their drunken fits, street arabs now enjoy hot slipper baths at the rate of one penny each, towel given in.'

Penning these words in 1906 he recalled that fifteen years earlier the stranger was warned not to venture alone into the neighbourhood and even the police patrolled in pairs. Now, instead of cut-throats these same streets were thronged with working-class harriers training for next Saturday's cross-country run. One evening as Paton approached the club and heard a din from inside a police officer said to him, 'You're raking the work off our hands, sir.' As Paton put it, he hit the point exactly. 'Either you must use forcible repression, or you must have increased opportunities for social life and healthy physical acitivity. Either our large towns must multiply police stations or multiply Boys' Clubs.'

These beliefs deeply coloured his attitude to the Manchester Grammar School. 'It is the nobility of the common people that is the salvation of the State,' he told his pupils, 'and it is the high tone of the rank and file of a school that is the salvation of that school.' Like an Old Testament prophet he urged the masters and boys to 'Uphold the good name of your school; keep the tone high; set your faces like flint against anything that is low or unworthy of your school; cut it down, sweep it away; overcome evil with good; turn bad to good, and better good with best, so that we may be able to claim for our school in this great city what the prophet of old claimed for the ideal city of his vision – that she is an eternal excellency and a joy for many generations.' Great though its achievements in the past, the Manchester Grammar School had never heard such a stirring call.

Hand in hand with such views about the nobility of the common people went Paton's disrespect for the distinguished and privileged private schools of England. Our 'boasted Public Schools' as he called them had, he perceived, been 'shut off from all contact with any but the monied classes' and with anyone else for all he could see. Their teachers were inbred, for public schools were largely staffed by ex-public schoolboys. A public schoolmaster, in

Paton's disapproving view, instead of spending his holidays at some East End settlement, went on furlough with like-minded, blinkered men. 'In fact, he never gets away from his Alma Mater's apron strings.' All this had contributed to the deplorable 'unreceptivity' and 'self-complacent stagnation' of a public school education. Such schools, he insisted, clung to what is old for the sake of its oldness, out of touch with the community they were supposed to serve.

In its place Paton proposed – and at Manchester set about to create – a school that would teach a boy 'something of what it means to be a member of a society in which the efficiency and good name of the whole are felt to depend upon the efficiency and honourable conduct of each constituent member,' a school which worked in an atmosphere of comradeship, training character 'by the best of all training, the responsibilities of leadership.'

Although Paton was convinced that 'the normal education must be for our country, as for all civilised countries, the Day School,' he generously acknowledged his debt to the public school, in particular to Thomas Arnold's Rugby. There Arnold had instituted a system of prefects, and Paton at Manchester adopted the same system. 'These sixth form boys or prefects, are to the headmaster what the scouting frigates are to Lord Nelson – they are the eyes of the fleet,' he wrote. 'It is this sixth form system which trains Englishmen in the art of government and the management of men,' said Paton. He also perceived the school hierarchy as a preparation for a boy's future life. 'The boy who can govern others at school grows up into the man

*The MGS rises in stark contrast to the buildings facing it, in this 1915 photograph.*

95

who can govern a province of India.'

Teaching the classics had an indispensable role in Paton's vision of a school at the service of a great nation and empire. Writing in 1897 on the teaching of Latin he had suggested that a man or woman's mental development exactly epitomizes the history of the human race. 'The schoolboy between the ages of 11 and 17 is just about in the same relative state of development as the Romans represented in the history of mankind,' he believed, both Romans and schoolboys at their best sharing the same qualities: 'a strong sense of discipline and patriotism, admiration for strength and all-round manliness, a shrewd, practical common sense intolerant of theorising, a strong feeling for the real and concrete, just awakening to the truths of generalisation and abstraction under the influence of their schoolmasters, the Greeks.' So modern Latin masters should seize the opportunity not to produce Latin specialists but to form taste, to teach boys to admire rightly. Learning Latin was in Paton's view an education in civic duty, for he believed that 'In no people as a whole do we find such firmness, courage, and above all such a strong sense of social obligation, as among the Romans.' For this reason Roman history should be familiar to the English-speaking boy from his earliest years, 'for nowhere else can he learn so well the sense of dignity and command which befits an imperial people, or that subordination of the individual to the community which we call public spirit.'

In 1903 the Manchester Grammar School looked with fascination at its new thirty-nine year old High Master. 'He believes in hard work, but at the same time is quite alive to the value of play,' *Ulula* had observed on Paton's arrival. 'The school athletics are not likely to suffer under his rule.' Paton begged the boys and masters to transfer to him all the affection they evidently felt for Mr King. In a trice the new High Master made it clear to the school that a man had come among them. 'What I ask of you,' he instantly demanded, 'is your hearty co-operation – masters and boys – that we may build worthily on that foundation which is laid, and build – not wood, hay, stubble, perishable things – but that which is pure, manly, and noble, and of good report, and which will endure in its turn the test of time.'

Not surprisingly, religion and in particular the daily assembly at the Manchester Grammar School played a central role in Paton's mission there. His father in 1906 had told one of his Anglican allies, the Bishop of Ripon, that in every school 'there should be, at 9 o'clock, a brief devotional service, with a hymn and a brief prayer, which would give the keynote to the whole of the morning's work, and would give the right tone to the minds of both scholars and teacher.'

At Manchester Paton was almost invariably present at morning prayers in the main school and (as a pupil recalled) usually read among other prayers the third collect for matins from the Book of Common Prayer. 'His hawk-like profile, piercing eyes, rubicund face and clear distinction with an accent on the r's – "neitherr rrun into any kind of dangerr" – together form a memory that does not fade.' Then lessons would start, though time would be found for members of the Scripture Union to hear a local clergyman speak perhaps on the text 'Seek ye first the kingdom of God and his righteousness' or to emphasise the importance of acquiring a thorough knowledge of the scriptures.

Curiously enough, the theological reasoning of this highly intelligent High Master was far from impeccable. He would lecture on the the subject 'Is Christianity true?', offering his hearers the choice between Jesus Christ or 'Another'. His simple-minded argument suggested, as alternatives to Jesus, D. G. Rossetti, Julius Caesar, Oliver Cromwell and the Nottingham poet Henry Kirke White. Paton briefly expounded the greatness of each of these men, only to find in each one some imperfection. Of Kirke White, for instance, he asked whether this man had the strength and manhood to stand up and rebuke sin or to lead against the powers of evil. 'Alas, no,' Paton judged. Then he turned to Jesus, in whom he found no fault at all. 'I only know one Master of the art of right living,' he continued. 'There is no inconsistency in that life, there is no gulf fixed between the public profession and the private life, there is no veil which you may not lift.' Jesus, he concluded, was 'a perfect example of righteous, godly, sinless life.' As Charles Lamb had once observed, so now did J. L. Paton: if William Shakespeare were to come into a room today we should all rise to our feet, but if Jesus of Nazareth were to come into the same room we should all fall on our knees.

Fortunately, a feeble theological argument does not detract either from the validity or the heartfelt strength of a person's religious faith. Paton's faith remained firm to the end, and he communicated it to countless boys.

First of all, however, he indulged his Germanic passion for the open air. Paton also revived the school's moribund rowing club. He founded a Whitsuntide cricket camp at Alderley Park, where little boys were given their first taste of living in tents. He loved camping, and soon he had established annual camps at Grasmere, where dressed in a grubby shirt, shorts and worn-out gym shoes he would be found cooking for the boys as they returned from climbing Langdale Pike and Helvellyn. During term-time the High Master himself would lead the pack in gruelling cross-country runs. When latrines needed digging, there was J. L. Paton wielding his spade, his trouser legs once again raised and kept in place by leather straps just below the knees.

The first Manchester Grammar School camp took place at Alderley Park in 1904, Paton and another master arriving by bicycle. Four tents and a marquee were pitched and the boys went to sleep. By six o'clock the following morning the lads of the advance party had all taken a dip in the mere and were ready to welcome the main group of forty-seven boys. Every day the High Master instructed seven new servants in washing up dishes, waiting at table, fetching water and bringing letters.

Entertainment included 'hickockalorumjig, French cricket and wrestling.' As the day ended the campers crowded round the camp fire, munching biscuits and singing songs. So these children of the owl learned the importance of helpfulness and diligence, stalking, cheerfulness and an awe-inspiring com-

*Proud parents and a shy boy at the Alderley Park camp, an institution founded at Whitsun in 1904.*

petence. Naturally the boys adored Scott of the Antarctic, and sent him a sledge for his last ill-fated journey to the South Pole.

Such good works were immeasureably magnified when, inevitably, Paton started a scout troop in the school. In 1910 he had himself led a large party of boys wandering and camping in the Taunus valley north of Frankfurt-am-Main. Two years later Paton set up the Manchester Grammar School scout troop. The way he set about it offers a fascinating vignette of his techniques of man-management. 'I attended the inaugural meeting of the scouts in 1912 chiefly to learn what it was all about,' recounted an assistant master named W. S. Dann. 'To my surprise J. L. Paton announced that I was to be one of the four Scoutmasters. I started therefore with no previous knowledge of scouting, in which I found that I differed little from my three colleagues.'

The following month one hundred boys gathered in the four corners of the gymnasium to form four troops of twenty-five members each. They found themselves scout huts in four Manchester suburbs, and soon on Saturday afternoons were to be seen in their light and dark blue jerseys, sky-blue neckerchiefs and smart scout hats. By September Paton had managed to engineer a visit to the school by the venerable Chief Scout himself, Baden Powell.

Careless of his public appearance, the man who could dig latrines with rolled up trouser legs once appeared at a dinner party at the Midland Hotel in Manchester dressed immaculately in tails and white tie, save for his brown boots.

98

In 1907 a pupil who had just left the school came upon his former High Master trudging across Kersal Moor. But for Paton's unmistakable figure and carriage he could have been taken for a tramp. 'He took me back home for tea,' the old Mancunian recalled, 'speaking humorously of his "disreputable appearance" as he called it, and told me how he had once been given a tip for holding a horse for a man who had, in fact, mistaken him for a tramp.'

This quaint yet formidable High Master cultivated the gift (or impression) of knowing every boy personally. In 1915 one of them was in Manchester Royal Infirmary, invalided from the North-West frontier eight years after he had left school. The first day he was allowed to walk out, he visited Long Millgate. There stood J. L. Paton. He saw his former pupil, crooked his finger and cried, 'Come in Johnny.' Although one of his successors, Lord James of Rusholme, was given to remark that any High Master claiming to know the names of every single boy in the school was a liar, somehow J. L. Paton pulled off the trick.

Long after his retirement from Manchester he met by chance on Preston railway station the Bishop of Sodor and Man who had been a pre-war pupil at the school. By now Paton was almost eighty years old but, as the bishop recalled, 'At once, he recognised me, though I had not seen him since he left Manchester, and was dressed as he had never seen me before, greeted me by my Christian name, said how glad he was about my Office and my work, enquired also by name of my two brothers, who had been at School with me, and of my parents and if they were yet alive.' The awestruck bishop concluded, 'And when he left the School there were 1,800 boys!' (This included the three preparatory schools).

He had in fact inherited a school of around 800 pupils. The subsequent increase in numbers led to ridiculously cramped conditions in Long Millgate, down which each day trundled drays loaded with cotton cloth and pulled by massive shire horses. The boys would pour out of their schoolrooms at break and rush across this narrow winding street to the tuck shop, to down a bottle of fizzy pop. Prefects dressed in mortar boards tried to keep down the noise. The older boys spent part of their spare time cramming away at classics or physics and chemistry. Occasionally a school football team would be excused the last lesson of the day and, under the stern eye of Jeppy, the venerable school porter since 1884, would take a tram to the playing fields near Higher Broughton or to the lacrosse, cricket and soccer pitches at Fallowfield.

The exertions of Paton's predecessors enabled him to indulge his zest for physical education. The *British Architect and Northern Engineer* had reported as early as 1877 that, 'Whilst venturing to hope that as regards mental education the Manchester School will bear comparison with any of our great schools, the trustees cannot but feel that it has hitherto been deficient in means of physical training – a matter of vital importance, especially in a town school. It cannot, they fear, be doubted that the physique of the boys, and indirectly also their mental powers, suffer for want of means of carefully directed bodily training.'

The school authorities in 1877 were convinced that gymnastics offered more

99

than a mere physical boost. 'A gymnasium will in part take the place of the field and the river as a means of promoting *esprit de corps* and community of feeling in the school,' they believed, as well as furnishing a spacious and airy place of resort during those intervals in the school work which hitherto had been wasted 'in lounging about the hall and corridors, to the detriment of good order, or in strolling about the streets of the city, at the risk of injury to both health and morals.'

These too were Paton's views But such pussyfooting remarks as those of 1877 paled beside his intense devotion to a healthy mind in a healthy body. 'A strong body is your servant; a weak body is your master,' he told the boys at his first Manchester Speech Day. 'See that you come back in September with strong bodies, ready for all the work you have got to do.' In all this he was worthily supported by, the school doctor Alfred A. Mumford, who loved to watch a new batch of boys on their first tentative days in the school gymnasium. He rejoiced to see 'the slouching shoulders, narrow chests and rounded backs, the apparently useless arms and the shuffling feet of the undeveloped boy give place – sometimes gradually and sometimes quickly – to erect attitude, properly placed shoulders, firm walk and alert glance.' Mumford was also a great one for making boys eat every morsel of the school dinner. As the master's minute book of 1 November 1923 records, the High Master had ordered that 'Any boy who is noticed to make a habit of leaving food will be sent to Dr Mumford, who had kindly undertaken to keep a supply of liquorice powder and castor oil to assist those whose digestion is weak.'

Another of Paton's educational aids was the birch, a long-tried standby of the High Masters of the Manchester Grammar School. Nicholas Germon had once beaten a boy so viciously that the dumbfounded onlookers feared that his victim would turn on the High Master and seize him by the throat. In the summer of 1907 a mother took J. L. Paton to court for birching her son on his bare bottom. Happily for Paton's sake the case was thrown out by the magistrates. Nonetheless the school doctor deemed it prudent to set out rules for such chastisements. 'CANING is the main punishment for small boys under 13 or 14,' his memo of 1914 declared, adding, 'Instrument for use – light cane, supplied by Mr Cox, approved by the Doctor.' The memorandum continued: 'The use of the cane is to cause a sharp sting of short duration. The abuse is to produce a bruise and haemorrhage under the skin. Note that it is by the bruising of subcutaneous tissues and nerves that the severity of punishment is judged under the law. Note also that "approval" by the doctor must not be construed to mean that no injury can result from the use of the cane so approved.' The memo concluded that adolescent boys aged fourteen and upwards needed special consideration, and that 'All cases of serious misconduct, lying, dishonesty, any form of impurity, flagrant disobedience, smoking, aggravated slackness or dissimulation, to be sent up to the H.M.' Then, in Paton's own words, he used his cane to 'reinforce the moral fibre of the boy'.

*'Jeppy': for fifty years between 1884 and 1934 Mr T. Jepson, the school porter, helped to keep the boys in order, doubling up as licensee of the nearby Manchester Arms.*

World War I aged him. In the years before its outbreak the school seemed to be preparing itself for some dreadful conflict. Forty-seven boys of the O.T.C. went to Aldershot in 1911, acquitting themselves well enough for the adjutant to laud them with the cry, 'Well done, Manchester, well done!' The following year over ninety O.T.C. boys camped out on Salisbury plain. The Manchester Grammar School was already training men ready to sacrifice themselves.

At Easter 1914 forty-seven members of the scout troop and a group of boys spent their holiday trekking in still peaceful Normandy. On 20 September a boy named Norman Birnage confided to his diary, 'At 3 o'clock I met Jones and we went for a walk. Then I said goodbye to him, for he is going to camp, probably for two months and then to the Front. He is getting a lieutenancy in the London fusiliers.' By October war had begun in earnest and *Ulula* was printing letters from Old Mancunians at the Front. 'I didn't like it at all,' W. H. Barratt wrote from Belgium. 'A chap next to me had his horse killed and one of our 20 was shot in the thigh, but we only lost 20 altogether, so their shooting was rotten. We were all in a chunk and they should have got at least half of us. We had 120 scouts in front on cycles, and only 30 came back, but our gunner killed several hundreds of the Germans. I was scared as anything.'

The roll of honour grew ominously longer. 'Loyal to his home, loyal to his school, loyal to his conscience and his highest duty, loyal in life, loyal in death – such was Edward Walsh,' the school magazine recorded in 1915. 'I have every reason to believe that his death was a quick one,' wrote Sergeant Webb, an Old Mancunian, about Frank Halliday, one of his former schoolfellows. Movingly, one of the dead was a German teacher, Dr Bernard Neuendorff, recruited by Paton and now fighting on the enemy side. Another was a French assistant who had taken up arms to defend his own country. Both names are inscribed on the school's 1914–1918 roll of honour.

The boys and staff did their bit for the war effort. As the Masters' Minute Book of February 1917 recorded, clearly the first duty of every teacher was to stick to his present work, though it was left to individual members of staff to decide whether they should take up national service during the holidays ('provided that it was such service as would bring the master back in renewed freshness of mind to his school work'). As for the boys, each one was urged to find some way of serving his country at half-term and weekends, either working as hospital orderlies, in YMCAs, or collecting paper, bottles and tin foil.

Paton's whole philosophy was based on a belief in progress. As a Christian he could not blindly embrace Darwinism with its materialistic overtones. Fortunately the so-called 'creative evolution' taught by Henri Bergson left a chink into which the influence of Paton's all-pervasive God might be inserted.

In 1921 and 1922 Olive A. Wheeler of Manchester University's department of education gave a series of lectures on the subject of Bergson and Education. Whereas Darwin's followers taught that 'evolution proceeds mechanically,' Bergson, she argued, believed in a vital impulse behind the process, 'something which ever seeks to transcend itself, to extract from itself more

*Still building: the 1913 addition rises to the left of 1870 school.*

than there is – in a word, to create.' This, both Bergson and Olive Wheeler held, was a spiritual force. It was a concept greatly appealing to J. L. Paton, and when the lectures were published he contributed a preface. Having listened to them, he wrote, 'They made clear and articulate to me what had hitherto been vague. I began to see the central increasing purpose which was expressing itself through our upward strivings.'

Education was thus for him an essential element in the progress of mankind. 'An educated man is a man who has been trained to conform to the law of progress,' was his creed. Progress, in his robustly Nonconformist view, depended on men and women being willing to question the *status quo*, in the way that for example Joan of Arc had refused to conform to the stereotyped woman of her era. His own notion of progress was also a moral one. Science he knew had made enormous strides during his own lifetime, but what of 'the triumphs of grace'? They were, he judged, still scanty. The spiritual element was lacking. 'If education is to change human nature and to keep on changing it in an upward direction, it must be spiritual; its methods must be spiritual; its atmosphere must be spiritual; its teachers must be spiritual men and women.' He wanted every child coming into a school to be treated 'first and foremost as a spiritual being.' Thus his school was allied to a dream of spiritual progress. Belief in the possibilities of progress was paramount in the scientific and medical world. 'We must believe in them with no less intensity in education,' declared J. L. Paton.

World War I failed to dent this belief. In 1919 Paton drew strength from a remark of Arnold Toynbee: 'It is well that the beaten ways of the world get trodden into mud; we are thus forced to seek new paths.' New things, Paton believed, were struggling to be born, and old things born again. 'We talk of

Reconstruction,' said the High Master. 'We should speak rather of Renaissance.' Men and women had forgotten the science of peace, he said. If they could but remember this science, 'the new world will come along the line of training and education.' Soon the Manchester Grammar School had founded a League of Nations Society, the High Master expressing his conviction of the benefits its growth would bestow on the school.

'Every boy is good for something,' was Paton's generous creed. He relished games, for, he judged that they had 'killed out in our Public Schools that bullying and those worse forms of self-indulgence which startle a modern reader in "Tom Brown" and Dr Anold's sermons.' But some boys were short-sighted or had weak hearts. Games were not for them. Instead the Manchester Grammar School under Paton directed these boys towards the Debating Society, the Natural History Society, the Camera Club, the Glee Club, the School Orchestra, the Chess Club, the Astronomical Society, the League of Nations Society and writing for the school magazine.

All of his boys, he hoped, would come under the insensible influence of a manly godliness. Rugby School and Socrates here joined forces in Paton's mind to promote this devout decency among his boys. Not much was said about religion at Shrewsbury (where he had been educated) or at Rugby (where he had taught) but he held that it flourished in the secret hearts of the boys themselves. 'There was no prayer meeting I ever heard of at Rugby or Shrewsbury,' he once wrote, 'but deep down there is the conviction that this, after all, is the one thing needful.' Paton recalled that, 'Even when there was the great rebellion at Rugby, and the headmaster was barred out of his own house, the sixth-form fellows held their regular prayers evening by evening.' As for Socrates, Paton would remind his boys and masters that when the

*A very early Grasmere camp, 1924.*

*PLATE 5 Pierre Adolphe Valette's 1910 painting of Albert Square, Manchester, depicts both an imposing city and the oppressive, smoky atmosphere which was eventually to persuade the school to move from Long Millgate to greener Fallowfield.*

young men came to ask him how they could combat the immorality that was rife in the city, Socrates replied that there was one simple word which could do all, the word κισϱον. 'Brand a bad thing as κισϱον, as "bad form," and at once you have enlisted the gregarious instinct definitely and decisively on the side of goodness.'

In 1924, after twenty-one years as High Master, Paton tendered his resignation to the governors. He told reporters that he was no longer at his best physically, adding firmly but cheerily, 'My governors have kindly suggested five month's holiday.' One reason for his resignation was that the school had finally decided to abandon Long Millgate and move to a site in Fallowfield. 'Noise, atmosphere, and lack of playing space have at last outweighed the ease with which it can be reached from all sides,' *Ulula* concluded in 1920. Paton welcomed the move as part of his beloved march to the music of progress. 'What was good enough for us would not be good enough for our sons,' he said, 'and we must try to face the fact that by moving to new quarters we were definitely improving the conditions under which our sons would be taught.' He also believed it only right that the new man who would have to run the school at Fallowfield should have some say about the shape of the new premises. As for his own future plans, 'I am going to kick my heels a bit before I decide,' he declared. 'I have no settled plans. There are no people like Manchester people, and I am sorry I cannot live with them for the whole of my days.'

'You may recharge an old battery, but it is still an old battery,' said the retiring High Master. 'I fear I am in the last decade of my allotted span.' In fact he lived for another twenty-two fruitful years, dying at Beckenham in Kent in 1946 at the age of eighty-two.

In the meantime after a year as a lecturer for the Canadian National Council of Education he became first president of the Memorial University College in St John's, Newfoundland. He retired in 1933, but took to teaching in a preparatory school in 1939, a job he was happily engaged in virtually till the day of his death.

At Manchester Paton had taught an *élite*. Yet he longed to 'put the best education within the reach of the humblest home', and continually urged governments and public school men to take their own *esprit de corps*, their traditions (and especially 'the same Christian manliness of character as they themselves had learned from the traditions of such great leaders and teachers as Thomas Arnold') into the education of all. When offered a knighthood and the CH, this doughty egalitarian declined, reputedly on the grounds that God had created so many ordinary, humble people that he must prefer them to the pompous and presumptuous. When he left Manchester over £4,000 was subscribed as a parting gift. Paton declined the money, directing that it be spent on enabling boys who could not otherwise afford it to go to camp.

When Paton set sail from Liverpool to Canada the school could not make up its mind whether it was saying goodbye to King Arthur or Dr Thomas Arnold. An aphorism written by Paton in the autograph book of a boy in the

PLATE 6

*Above: The book of remembrance in the school vestibule.*

*Above: The memorial figure above the main entrance to the hall. Above the statue a stained glass window bears the school coat of arms, and below it is the inscription* Comitum caesorum memores MCMXIV– MCMXVIII.

*Below: The King's colour of the 1st/6th battalion and the 2nd/6th battalion of the Manchester regiment with the regimental colour in the middle, in Manchester cathedral. Many old boys fought and died in these battalions at Gallipoli in 1915.*

*Below:* Pro patria mori: *the French and German teachers whose names were inscribed on the roll of honour when they died for their countries in the 1914–18 War.*

Lower School was quoted and requoted: 'The days that are gone we cannot recall them, and we should not wish to do. They were given us to ennoble the days that are and the days that are to come.' Was the unmistakable hint of King Arthur's farewell in Tennyson's *Idylls of the King* conscious or unconscious? Recalling their beloved High Master's words, as Paton left them in 1924 the schoolboys and masters of the Manchester Grammar School imagined themselves standing on the shore like Sir Bedivere, 'revolving many memories' as the once and future king sailed away, '"straining our eyes beneath an arch of hand," to see our late Leader passing "down that long water opening on the deep"; feeling quite certain, however, that he will be thinking of us while he is on the ocean, just as surely as we, in our thousands, shall be thinking of him.'

Rugby school was also in their minds. 'Those who visit Rugby, and read the instruction on the Arnold memorial there, are struck by the single word *fronte*,' said *Ulula*. 'We of Manchester also shall carry with us all through our lives the vision of an "ample brow," and a face on which a look of deep seriousness would often break suddenly into the sunniest of smiles, as its owner passed from some earnest appeal or scathing denunciation to those touches of irresistible humour that would send a whole assembly into rippling laughter.'

So J. L. Paton passed from Manchester to Canada, a blend of Dr Arnold and King Arthur, though – as a subsequent High Master put it – an Arthur decidedly without his Guinevere.

# 7

## Allegro ma non Troppo
## 1924–1989

MR Dougie Miller, said J. L. Paton, was the only man in the world of whom he was a bit jealous. Douglas Miller was Paton's successor at the Manchester Grammar School, and Paton prophesied that when in the far distant future Miller came to retire he too would be equally jealous of the High Master chosen to follow him.

Douglas G. Miller was a Scotsman, educated at Fettes College from which he gained a Postmastership (which means a senior scholarship) at Merton, Oxford's oldest college. An Oxford rugger blue, he somewhat neglected his academic work but took creditable seconds in mods and greats. His first job on going down was teaching at the Royal Naval College, Dartmouth, during which time he played for Devon and won his county cap. For one year he taught at Christ's College, Brecon, before going on to Uppingham, where for the next four years he was an extremely successful housemaster. In 1913 Dougie Miller became rector of Kelvinside Academy, Glasgow. Thirteen years later he was headmaster of Aberdeen High School.

*A Scotsman in charge: Dougie Miller, High Master, 1924–1945.*

This was a meteoric career. Yet these were not the only achievements that boded well for the Manchester Grammar School, for what entranced the boys and staff as they learned of his appointment was that he had also been capped five times for the Scottish Rugby XV. Shy, dour, invariably smoking a straight-stemmed pipe, he was a direct man. Some took his gentleness for weakness, till the more perspicacious spotted how skilfully he had welded together a harmonious team of sharp-witted teachers. He loved Scotland, and initially refused the invitation to come south to Manchester. The governors pressed him and he relented. Unfortunately this splendidly fit man now began to experience indifferent health, so that Douglas Miller's years as High Master were clouded with illness, although he was coaching the new boys in rugger in 1933.

His first major task was to ease the rigorous timetable of the Paton years. Boys under Miller's regime worked a six period day, not a day of five periods, so that each class lasted only fifty minutes instead of an arduous hour. This was reduced to forty-five minutes on moving to Rusholme. Miller's second major task was to supervise the long-projected move from Long Millgate to Fallowfield. The architects of the new school, Percy Worthington and Francis Jones Jr, were gifted men. Worthington especially had been responsible for some notable buildings, but at the Grammar School their flair was not much in evidence. They built a brick, subdued neo-Georgian building at a cost of

*Goodbye: locking up the old school for the last time.*

107

£240,000. It was adorned with a statue of the founder by William McMillan. By a rainy September in 1931 the boys and masters were installed in an unaccustomed new home. As usual in such affairs, the official opening was delayed. Lord Derby arrived at Fallowfield on 17 October. The sun had pierced the gloom. Worthington and Jones gave him a golden key. He walked down the long drive between two ranks of staff, formally opened the main door, entered the memorial hall and unveiled a statue to Hugh Oldham.

Over 1,100 boys crammed themselves into new buildings designed for no more than 950. By the end of World War II the numbers had reached nearly one and a half thousand. The new school boasted a Great Hall one hundred and ten feet long and panelled in English oak, a woodwork room, a museum, an ample lecture room 'designed also for theatricals and kinematograph', a massive art room, a gymnasium and a parade ground. Since the school was nonetheless still too small, Douglas Miller's time as High Master saw cellars converted into temporary classrooms. Even so, shortly after he had left the school science masters were obliged to teach in prefabricated laboratories.

Now the Manchester Grammar School introduced one of its most distinctive features: an incredibly short working day. Miller realised that boys could no longer arrive to start school at 9.05 in the morning. They also needed to get home in the hours of daylight. The Manchester Grammar School Day changed, beginning now at 9.30 a.m. and ending at a quarter to four in the afternoon.

Yet the corporate life of the school remained unimpaired. As Miller himself put it, 'I have often noticed in accounts of school gatherings the tacit assumption that a vigorous corporate life can only be enjoyed in a boarding school. This seems to me a strange and fantastic idea. When you consider the day school of today, and the Manchester Grammar School in particular, all the societies which we run, all the games we play, our A.T.C., our treks and camps, and even the common meal in the dining hall, it seems to me just foolish to suggest a corporate life cannot be carried out in a day school.'

This corporate life was undoubtedly fostered by the fact that the school at last had playing fields on its own doorstep. The High Master's own prowess at Rugby meant that this game began to rival football and lacrosse at Manchester. In the 1937–38 season the rugger team beat eighteen out of twenty-six other XVs, the soccer team won eighteen out of twenty-four matches and the lacrosse team defeated twenty-six of its thirty opponents. To the school's delight, an old boy named Bert Toft became captain of the English Rugby XV.

Less active pursuits included a passion among some boys for the supposedly iconoclastic music known as jazz. *Ulula* in 1930 carried a defence of jazz aimed at those who claimed that through this savage music 'the old classical idea of wine, women and song has been destroyed by the passion for hooch, sin and syncopation.' As the boy succinctly argued, 'Jazz outrages the laws of conventional music simply because it is unconventional music,' astutely adding that '*vers libre* was sneered at when it first made its appearance.'

*Royal congratulations for Bert Toft, old boy, captain of the England Rugby team and master 1932–1939.*

Corporate life was matched by academic excellence. Under Miller the school maintained its pre-eminence in training boys for the ancient universities. Sixteen Oxford open scholarships in 1926 and seventeen in 1929 testified to the quality of the staff Miller had inherited and the brains of the boys entering his school (many of them of course from its three feeder preparatory schools). In 1934 the Board of Education reported that the Manchester Grammar School had in the previous three years won seventy Oxbridge scholarships, sixty-six places at the university of Manchester and sixteen at other universities. More and more gifted boys applied to become pupils at the school, till the numbers pressing to join became almost embarrassing.

In August 1939 Miller had a new problem to tackle. Faced with the prospect of Britain declaring war against Germany, the school was asked to evacuate its boys from Manchester to Blackpool. By the beginning of the following month Germany had invaded Poland. The next day was a Saturday and nearly 800 boys, masters and masters' wives met at the school, marched out in orderly fashion, boarded buses which took them to Victoria station and clambered aboard a train for Blackpool, carrying their gas masks in cardboard boxes. One third of the school simply stayed at home.

At Blackpool the evacuees set up camp on Marton Moss, At eleven o'clock in the evening the heavens opened. Parts of the camp were under six inches of water. On Sunday the whole school was miserable. Blankets were folded, and after breakfast everyone was shipped off in buses to the Palatine Road Central School. There boys, masters and masters' wives were told they would have to sleep on bare floors. Lunch was provided in relays at a Blackpool restaurant. No work was done, but as the days passed the boys were farmed out to

*Abandoning its roots, the school departs for Blackpool on 2 September 1939.*

*Unfamiliar surroundings: parents, masters and boys stand bewildered on Marton Moss, Blackpool.*

various respectable Blackpool homes. Books were procured from Manchester and paper from Woolworths, yet schoolwork was a disaster. No-one could find any chalk. The Palatine Road Central School could accommodate the boys and staff only during the mornings in one week and the afternoons in the next. Parents began to recall their boys home, enrolling them in other schools.

Miller, Mr T. F. Nutter, who was the Receiver, and Sir Arthur Haworth, Chairman of the Governors, saw the writing on the wall. The three of them travelled to London to bend the ear of Lord Woolton, an old Mancunian who was now Minister of Food. Woolton pulled the necessary strings, and the school was permitted to return home, with the proviso that adequate air raid shelters should be built around the buildings and the staff were all to be trained as air raid wardens.

The air raid precaution chief in Manchester was enraged at the reopening. The School governors cared not a whit for his views. Asked if the school was encouraging others to abandon their safe havens, Sir Arthur Haworth replied, 'No, we are not leading a retreat or giving a bad example.' As one participant in these stirring events remembered, 'The news that we were to come home was received with a wild joy – most of us felt that when we got back to M.G.S. we would wander around and around the School, just looking at it.' In 1942 as a thank-offering to Lord Woolton, his fellow old Mancunians presented him with a finely carved wooden owl. Woolton for his part promised to give a new carpet for the chapel of Hugh Oldham in Exeter cathedral, but new restrictions on wool stopped the plan.

Unfortunately the school did not emerge unscathed from this transfer back to Manchester. Air raids on 22 and 23 December, 1940, destroyed the 'Owl's Nest' campsite at Disley, as well as half the old building in Long Millgate which still belonged to the governing body. A landmine fell in the school grounds – happily on a Saturday when no boys were present, though it

*The skeleton of the 1880 building after the December blitz, 1940.*

demolished doors, glass and window-frames. Then on 1 January 1941, another landmine dropped on Withington, falling behind a group of patrolling air raid wardens. One of them was one of the school's most beloved masters, Hyman Lob. Not a trace of him or any of his fellow wardens remained. He was fifty-five years old.

Hyman Lob (or Harry Lob as everyone called him) had become a

111

*The new school narrowly escaped destruction when a bomb fell on the school playing fields in 1940.*

*Harry Lob (MGS 1908–1941) remembered for his compassion and tireless devotion to the school.*

Manchester Grammar School institution. A Londoner, he had joined the staff in 1908 as a Cambridge mathematics graduate. Six years later Lob was at war, serving in France with the 8th Battalion East Lancs Regiment and then with the Royal Engineers. Demobilised, he returned to his school which he was to serve for thirty-two years. 'Think of "trekking" and you thought of Lob,' wrote the *Manchester Guardian* after his death; 'talk of "under 14" cricket or football and you spoke of Lob; discuss school music and you discussed Lob.' Lob was also a scholar, and one who cared for the weaker boys. 'He could feel for the simplest difficulty of the Tiniest Tim,' it was said. His mild eyes, peering through spectacles over a particularly foul pipe which champed in his mouth, oozed kindliness. He never went to bed before the small hours, was late for every meal, and as a devout Jew laboured tirelessly for the victims of Nazism. He cared also for the poor. As a Christian clergyman testified after Lob's death, small boys from poor homes were able to get onto a school team because Harry gave them tram fares and begged shirts for them. 'His name will crop up frequently at the firesides of Old Mancunians for many years to come,' declared the Revd T. J. Jeans. 'We cannot say that we have lost him, for the spirit of Lob will remain as long as there are boys to teach in Manchester.' One of his fellow ARP wardens looked back on their hours tramping through the streets together, while Lob recounted endless amusing anecdotes, as 'walking through fairy-land.' He saluted his dead friend, 'Goodbye, Mr Chips-in-the-Flesh!'

The boys' war effort was prodigious. They picked fifty tons of potatoes, plucked and pressed peas, cut down trees and sorted and delivered letters. For

Dougie Miller these were years of deep sorrow. The first old boy to be lost at sea was his youngest son. Soon another son was a German prisoner of war. The whole school again went through the misery of hearing the names of old boys – over 200 of them – who had been killed in action. Increasingly wracked with sickness, Miller was determined to stay at his post until the conflict was over. In 1945 he gratefully laid down the burden of office.

As he said good-bye to the school in the Palace Theatre, Manchester, (for the Free Trade Hall had been blitzed) 1,300 voices sang the stirring lilt and nostalgic words of 'The Road to the Isles'. Douglas Miller's parting words to the boys expressed his feeling of privilege at having shared for twenty-one years in a great comradeship. He did not need to point out that in 1944 the school had won 37 open scholarships at Oxford and Cambridge, beating its own previous record of 23. 'That together we have achieved some success is cause for satisfaction,' he confessed, 'but to me the overwhelming feeling is one of gratitude for the constant understanding and helpful kindliness that I have received from all, the Boys, the Masters, the School Staff, the Old Mancunians.' In his place, he declared, was to come 'a man of great ability, one who, from my personal knowledge of him will quickly establish himself in your affections.' That man was Dr Eric John Francis James.

He was in his thirty-sixth year, and had been educated at Taunton's School, Southampton, and as a scientist at the Queen's College, Oxford (which had recognised his brilliance by transforming his exhibition into an honorary scholarship). Since 1933 he had been an assistant master at Winchester College. To be appointed to Manchester was, he recalled, 'my idea of bliss. I had always wanted to be the headmaster of a day school.' Though a southerner, he

*Eric James, apostle of meritocracy, High Master 1945–1961.*

*A fateful meeting. On 26 April 1945 the governors decided to appoint Eric James as Dougie Miller's successor.*

grew to love the north of England. 'Is it possible for anyone to live in Manchester?' asked a young upstart being interviewed by James for a teaching post at the school. 'Yes,' the High Master replied, 'but not you.'

At Manchester he inherited problems. The school was hard up. Its buildings had been bombed. Wartime had meant the employment of temporary and in some cases inefficient staff. Morale was low. Miller, tired and arthritic, had in his last years as High Master not really been tough enough for Manchester, though Eric James regarded him as a marvellous man who had never been given the credit he deserved.

The new High Master knew precisely what sort of school he wished to create in the post-war age. His intention was that the Manchester Grammar School should be able to boast that it was open to any boy of sufficient ability, whatever his background. Dr James perceived the preparatory schools as anomalous institutions, feeder schools which seemed to infiltrate boys into the Grammar School by the back door. He therefore closed them down, selling them to the local authority. James planned to make his school 100 per cent selective. His policy caused some hard feelings, especially among such old boys as assumed their sons had an automatic right of entry. 'I regret to say that I was a bit rigid,' said James later in life, 'but the regret is slight.'

The direct grant system gave precisely the Goverment help his policy needed. It was, he declared, 'the ideal system of school government. It places the school within the state system, and yet leaves it independent. It enables us to grade our fees according to the parents' income.' By 1961 55 per cent of the boys were having their fees paid by the local education authorities. Although the other 45 per cent nominally paid fees, if their parents' incomes were low, these fees too could be waived. 'Are you poor?' the High Master would ask parents, commenting if the answer was yes, 'Fine: the poorer, the better.' In consequence the Manchester Grammar School had never been so socially accessible. Since it was not governed by one local education authority but related to no fewer than fifteen, it was also geographically accessible. The only test was merit. Late each February between 1,500 and 2,000 small boys would arrive from the Manchester conurbation and beyond to sit the entrance exam. Some 200 passed. It was, as Eric James claimed, 'a highly selective entry system which yet produced a school incredibly mixed socially. That,' he once affirmed, 'is our greatest glory.'

James believed that England stood on the edge of a genuine social revolution. Two years after arriving at the school he claimed that he and his colleagues 'were attempting a task that had never been attempted before: to give an education to a whole democracy.' He told the Old Mancunians that when he looked through his study window he had no idea whether the boy dropping an ice-cream paper came from a home where the income was £4 a week or a home whose income ran into four figures.

Eric James was also deliberately training these boys for leadership in a democratic society. He knew that, as he put it, 'The whole idea of leadership is viewed with a healthy suspicion in democratic communities.' To be acceptable, leadership now needed to be based on persuasion instead of arbitrary decision, on demands which can be seen to be intrinsically reasonable. He also argued that 'in practice, if not always very frankly in theory, the necessity of high intelligence for leadership has been admitted for a long time.' Yet although he held high intellectual capacity to be without doubt the first quality called for in a leader, James insisted that other temperamental and moral qualities were no less vital. These he defined as 'integrity, courage, judgment, stability, tact and perseverance.' Above all leadership in a democratic society must, like his school, 'be open to merit'.

James called on John Stuart Mill ('as great a defender of true democracy as ever lived') and Plato in his support. He quoted Mill's argument that, 'No government by a democracy. . . either in its political acts or in the opinions, qualities and tone of mind which it fosters, ever did or could rise above mediocrity, except in so far as the sovereign Many have let themselves be guided (which, in their best times they always have done) by the counsels and influence of a more highly gifted and instructed One or Few.' As for Plato, writing 'the greatest of all books on education' the Athenian philosopher had seen that the teaching of the future Guardians was the noblest of all occupations. 'Against the background of the twentieth century,' said James in 1960, 'we can see how right he was'.

Eric James had inherited some splendid teachers to train his future guardians: 'Taffy' Hughes, who taught chemistry; Albert Hislop, whom James promoted to second master; F. L. Heywood, a genius as head of mathematics who, James agreed, 'was so devoted to scholarship that he got us a bad name as a cramming establishment'; and a brilliant linguist named John Lingard. His own recruits included Roger Young, later to run George Watson's School, Edinburgh, where he received a knighthood, and Roy Cooke, later to become Director of the Coventry Schools.

'The secret of success is to surround yourself with very able men, and take credit for what they do,' said James. 'That's what I did.' He himself, though often absent promoting and defending his kind of education, still managed to teach sixth formers Plato's *Republic*. He also taught chemistry to a sixth form B stream, since to take the best boys would have been unfair on his colleagues. And he tried to ensure that his school had the finest tools, most obviously obtaining £50,000 from an old boy, Sir Simon Marks, and another £5,000 from Simon Marks' brother-in-law Israel Sieff, to add another storey to the science block and a lecture theatre.

Music, he eventually decided, was 'terrible' and the school choir 'a disgrace'. Towards the end of his time as High Master he managed to persuade the cricket enthusiasts on the staff to let him use the long room of their pavilion as a music centre and appointed 'a ball of fire' named David Cawthra as a music master. Soon the school musicians were able enough to play Verdi's *Requiem*.

He also set about humanising the school, with drama and with pictures, as well as encouraging the long tradition of camps and treks. 'We make the error of laying too much emphasis on actual team games,' he said, 'for greater

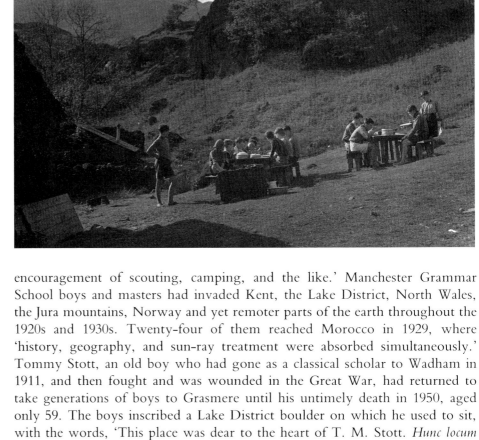

Right: *Manchester Wandervögel: Grasmere in the 1930s.* Above: *The Grasmere barn, a haven for generations of campers.* Below: *A boy plays the cello seated on the boulder loved by Tommy Stott, master from 1920–1950.*

encouragement of scouting, camping, and the like.' Manchester Grammar School boys and masters had invaded Kent, the Lake District, North Wales, the Jura mountains, Norway and yet remoter parts of the earth throughout the 1920s and 1930s. Twenty-four of them reached Morocco in 1929, where 'history, geography, and sun-ray treatment were absorbed simultaneously.' Tommy Stott, an old boy who had gone as a classical scholar to Wadham in 1911, and then fought and was wounded in the Great War, had returned to take generations of boys to Grasmere until his untimely death in 1950, aged only 59. The boys inscribed a Lake District boulder on which he used to sit, with the words, 'This place was dear to the heart of T. M. Stott. *Hunc locum multum amavit.*' For over two decades another old boy, G. I. S. Bailey, returned as a teacher after his days at Merton, trekked with boys in his beloved Scotland.

What James refused to encourage was the Hugh Oldham Lads' Club. Slum clearance had drastically reduced the number of attenders. But for half a century Grammar School boys had camped at Penmaenmawr or Prestatyn with working class boys from the club. Masters and boys had habitually visited Livesey Street, playing billiards and inspecting the bathrooms and the club reading rooms. The Lads' Club harriers and cricket team had regularly played against the school. Preparatory school boys and grammar school boys had annually made a collection for the club. The club's Nigger Minstrel singers were regularly winning prizes in local competitions.

'We who live out of the city in healthy homes, on wholesome food, with

116

*The Dramatic Society's production of Molière's* That Scoundrel Scapin *in February 1958. Robert Powell (right) plays the title role; Ben Kingsley appeared in the same production.*

plenty of holidays, cannot by any power of the imagination picture to ourselves the delight of these lads when they go off to camp,' one boy wrote in *Ulula* after a trip with the Lads' Club to Rossall, near Fleetwood. Eric James regarded all this as out-of-date, admirable in its day but no longer relevant. 'I wanted to see those boys in the Manchester Grammar School, not in a lads' club,' he explained. He summarily closed the club down, though he kept going the annual charity collection which now went to what the High Master regarded as better causes.

Some of these were major changes; yet his mark as High Master was supremely one of academic discipline. The brightest of the boys in an exceptionally bright school found their O levels pared down to the bare minimum – English, a foreign language and mathematics – to qualify them for university entrance. They then streaked ahead for A levels.

Eric James, knighted in 1956 and created a life peer in 1959, wrote and spoke a great deal on the dangers of over-specialisation and made strenuous efforts at Manchester to teach some humanities to boys on the science side and some science to non-scientists. Neither an egalitarian nor a conformist, he longed to teach heretics, for, he believed, 'The heretic may ultimately be the best citizen.' Eric James had no desire to train Manchester School boys as supine conformists.

In his fight for academic standards, he found himself more and more a heretic in an egalitarian world, for soon his beloved grammar schools were under threat, even though initially few among the new Labour Ministers were opposed to them. Eric James fought hard, intellectually and politically, against

117

the comprehensive school ideal. Its advocates claimed that comprehensive education mitigated the strains and rigidities of selection at eleven or twelve, and instead created a more unified society. Eric James claimed otherwise. Comprehensive education, he argued, actually promoted class divisions by replacing the socially and geographically wide system of grammar school selection with an intake from a geographically limited area. More, he was convinced that 'from the point of view of . . . the education of the most able, there is no doubt that the comprehensive high school presents very serious difficulties'. In Manchester he met Lady Sheena Simon, whom he came to dub 'a dear friend, a beloved enemy, apostle of comprehensive schools.' As he recalled, 'we spent many a happy evening fighting each other.'

He and teachers of like mind lost both this fight and the fight to save the direct grant. It was abolished by a socialist Minister of Education who was later to abandon the Labour party. 'My proudest boast was that the Manchester Grammar School is within the State system and available to anyone,' James later said ruefully. 'It always was until Shirley Williams got her claws into it.'

After sixteen years as High Master Lord James of Rusholme was offered the Vice-Chancellorship of the fledgling University of York. The job was too tempting to refuse, and he left Manchester. His successor was a man of a quite different stamp, Mr Peter Mason.

Peter Geoffrey Mason's academic career was distinguished, a foundation scholar of King Edward's School, Birmingham, who became a major scholar of Christ's College, Cambridge, taking a first in both parts of the classical tripos and becoming Porson university scholar. He had taught and been a housemaster at Cheltenham College, and during the Second World War had been commissioned into the Intelligence Corps. Before returning to education he worked in the foreign office and was awarded the MBE. Then he went to Rugby as lower bench master, leaving there to become headmaster of Aldenham School.

The new High Master was thus a man steeped not in the day school tradition but in the ways of public schools. On arriving at Manchester Peter Mason was surprised to find two questions continually put to him by the staff he had inherited: What do you think of Lancashire? and, Aren't boarding schools a bad thing?

What he thought about his new home was that it was in danger of becoming aggressively parochial. The calibre of his staff was extremely high; a very selective entry brought to the school boys of high academic ability who in turn attracted men who wanted to teach at that level; but, Peter Mason recalled, 'Manchester Grammar School was a place to which people came for education, not a community as I understood it.' He wanted to humanise the place, to improve the boys' social behaviour, their dress and their discipline. He succeeded.

He also felt that heads of department took hold of boys far too early and decided whether they were to become classicists or scientists. For some time a

*Peter Mason, High Master from 1962 to 1978, who steered the school through dangerous years of political controversy.*

118

number of Oxbridge tutors, however unfairly, had come to look upon boys from the school as the victims of too much cramming, who arrived at university as burnt-out cases. 'We have all been irritated from time to time by the accusation that MGS is a hot-house for meritocrats, a well oiled machine for getting large numbers by early specialisation into Oxbridge and the higher reaches of the academic and professional world,' wrote R. W. Baldwin, the Chairman of the Governors. 'This was always a travesty of the truth, but one of Peter Mason's chief contributions has been the even greater emphasis placed on the broadest possible education.' Mason ensured that even in the sixth form the boys devoted a third of their time to non-examination subjects.

In no way did this mean a diminution in the school's academic excellence. '*The Case for Super-Schools* is the title of one of Peter Mason's published articles, and nobody has any doubt that Manchester Grammar School is super,' a journalist observed in 1976, adding that 'if you felt you had to defend bestness against hostile critics, you would start with MGS, whose bestness is somehow both incontrovertible and defensible.'

Peter Mason was a tall man and like Lord James also of commanding presence, and given to hospitality. Monica Furlong, the journalist, who came to interview him in 1969 was received in a large room with a glowing coal fire and offered an excellent glass of sherry out of a Wine and Food Society bottle. 'He is a very big man, with curling white hair and the quiet confidence habitual to giants,' she reported. 'His colleagues refer to him as "the Chief" and the title suits him.' She continued, 'He seems a little apart from the hurly-burly, yet shrewdly aware of it, peering benevolently down,' a description that could have been applied equally well to Lord James of Rusholme.

Peter Mason differed from his predecessor in being a devout Anglican, whereas Eric James had remained robustly agnostic, though, like many an agnostic headmaster, perfectly willing if asked to preach his stimulating views from Christian pulpits. As headmaster of Aldenham, Peter Mason had been proud to oversee the completion of the school chapel and the acquisition of a new boarding house. At Manchester he tried and failed both to found a boarding house (though some old boys were constantly demanding one) or to buy Birch church, when it fell vacant, to serve as a school chapel. He did manage to transform morning assembly into a normal public school service, with far more visiting speakers. He instituted a termly service of Holy Communion, and he appointed a school chaplain.

He soon found himself with a yet more difficult task on his hands, and one crucial to the survival of his school. The Labour Party was making increasingly clear its intention to destroy the direct grant system. Even before it came to power, its allies in local government were already attempting to persuade primary school heads not to put forward their bright boys for places at the Grammar School. Peter Mason was convinced not only academic excellence was in danger of wanton destruction for political ends; he also felt that few realised how fragile this excellence was and how difficult it would be to recreate if it were ever lost.

*The clock tower presented by Owen Cox, the school's receiver 1888–1934. The initials OCR are seen at 3, 6, 9, and 12.*

119

*The old rectory of Birch church, Rusholme, now the biology department.*

Initially he spent many weary and frustrating hours trying to defend the system he had inherited. Eric James had been fond of saying that the Minister of Education was his boss. Peter Mason saw the need for a new philosophy. 'It became clear to me that direct grant schools were independent schools with a contract with the Government,' he said. 'If that status disappeared, the deluge would come.' His efforts and those of like-minded educationalists met with increasing hostility. When the High Master and Raymond Baldwin, Chairman of the Governors, went to put to those in charge of education at Manchester town hall the many advantages of such schools as theirs, they were met with the frosty remark, 'Anything you can do, we can do better.'

It was, Peter Mason recalled, 'a tiresome period'. Increasingly his bulletins to parents and his newsletters to the Old Mancunians became preoccupied with what the High Master called educational politics. It soon became clear to him that an entirely new pattern of funding the academically bright children of poorer families was required, if they were still to be educated in independent schools. It was also clear that in playing a leading role in setting up such a scheme, educational politics would occupy more and more of his time. Peter

PLATE 7

*Above: The Fallowfield buildings to which the Manchester Grammar School moved in 1931 were designed by Percy Worthington and Francis Jones (Jnr). The school had been unable to sell the Long Millgate buildings and so the new buildings were to be functional rather than lavish. The front of the school where the art hall windows can be seen on either side of the school's coat of arms.*

*Above: The High Master's entrance in the main quadrangle; the Pennines can be seen in the distance.*

*Below: The sports pavilion completed in 1956 was built to commemorate those old boys who gave their lives in the Second World War.*

*Below: The school weather vane; a master endlessly pursues, but never catches, a recalcitrant boy.*

PLATE 8

*Above: Bust of Frederick William Walker (High Master 1859–77) by Bruce Joy. Presented to the school in 1907.*

*Below: Practice at the school's new organ, built by Peter Collins.*

*Above: A memorial to a revered High Master, J. L. Paton cast in bronze by John Cassidy.*

*Below: Two of the charges from the school's coat of arms, in elaborate carving in front of the organ pipes.*

Mason therefore restructured the chain of command in his school. Two surmasters were appointed, to run the school in his absence. The scheme worked perfectly. As one observer put it, 'When the Captain is ashore (and even when he isn't) his two staff Captains are pacing the bridge, scanning distant horizons, and giving imperceptible but perfectly judged alterations to the helm.'

The Manchester Grammar School was so run that in Monica Furlong's words, 'streamlined efficiency seems to run through the place like warm water.' It was an efficiency that enabled the High Master to accept more and more time-consuming offices, and above all as vice-chairman of the Headmasters' Conference Direct Grant Joint Committee to put forward a plan for financially assisted places at independent schools which in 1972 became the official policy of the Conservative opposition party. With delicious irony an educational journalist noted that 'What everyone knows about the High Master is that he presides over the academically most successful school in the world, and is away from it more than any other headmaster.'

Had Peter Mason not been away so much, his school might have lost its unique, precious character. As well as creating the assisted places scheme virtually single-handed, he tirelessly searched for other funds. The Old Mancunians were wooed and responded magnificently. At a cost of nearly £200,000 the school swimming baths were remodelled. In 1965 Queen Elizabeth II arrived to open a new sixth form block. In his years as High Master parents, Old Mancunians, businessmen and other supporters eventually contributed more than a million pounds to the school. When he resigned he left a thriving and independent school which had once looked more and more vulnerable to the tyrannical control of an unsympathetic state.

*The Queen's visit in 1965.*

121

*An era of transition: the school under David Maland between 1978 and 1985, broadened its curriculum dramatically and early specialisation came to an end.*

*Work in silver done in the CDT department.*

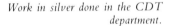

'If the case for freedom of choice and variety so vitally important for the preservation of democracy and individual liberty in an increasingly pluralistic society is, as the evidence suggests, so generally agreed in the Western world,' he insisted, 'it is hard to avoid the conclusion that we in Britain should widen rather than further restrict access to British private schools by transferring some at least of the cost of private education to public funds.' Private education was an institution which he believed played a vital role in a free society, contributing through successive generations of boys its own liberal ethos to an adult, democratic citizenship.

His successor as High Master added another thread to this pattern. For David Maland the major function of the private sector in education was not to offer unrivalled skills and experience or to seek to cultivate a profound religious ethos in a boy's upbringing – important though these elements were. He held that the image of such schools as 'beacons of light in a dark age' was a self-indulgent one. 'I prefer,' he said, 'the image of a gad-fly.' Independent schools were necessary because they offered a perpetual alternative to the provision made by the state. By their very existence they prevented the establishment of a state monopoly, a monopoly which would be the first step on the dangerous road towards a totalitarian society. They offered, he maintained, 'an indispensable safeguard against the drift towards totalitarian government by the Right or by the Left.'

David Maland was a Yorkshireman by birth, a national serviceman, a former assitant master at Brighton Grammar School, sometime head of history at Stamford School and successively head of Cardiff High School and Denstone College. A distinguished historian, his published works included *Europe in the Seventeenth Century, Culture and Society in Seventeenth Century France, Europe in the Sixteenth Century* and *Europe at War, 1600–1650.* At Manchester he found a school whose staff was so gifted and boys so highly-tuned that, as he later expressed it, the one task of a High Master was to keep out of everyone's way. He inherited, he said, not so much problems as opportunities. What he decided to do in fact was not so much to increase the pressure on boys as to slow it down.

An inspiration came from a member of staff at a common room meeting. The master observed that the school worked boys and staff so hard that he feared there was 'no time to gather flowers by the wayside'. As an historian David Maland also believed that subjects like his own needed a measure of maturity in scholars before they could be properly appreciated. Even though he had a staff perfectly capable of exciting boys about physics, French or history given sufficient time, no one could truly cram anyone into an understanding of history or indeed of physics. But change was hard to effect. At Denstone he had been able to switch directions by a gentle turning of the tiller, but the Manchester Grammar School seemed like a massive oil tanker that took half the ocean to turn around. The curriculum changes he wished to introduce took over one and a half years to take effect.

Paradoxically Oxford and Cambridge came to his aid. In the past, the two

122

ancient English universities had managed to exert a stifling hold over the grammar schools. F. W. Walker had told the Taunton commission in 1865 that he longed to abolish Greek and Latin verses from his school, save for those boys with a pronounced ability for philological studies – a course which, he added, 'I dare not do until the Universities take the lead.' So long as the universities required Latin verses for their scholarship, Walker intended to go on teaching the subject.

Later in the century Michael George Glazebrook had taken up the same theme in his 1890 presidential address on 'The Universities and specialisation' to the Manchester branch of the Teachers' Guild. 'If the university examinations injure the schools by debarring average boys from special studies, the colleges with their system of scholarships are continually tempting the cleverer boys into undue specialisation,' Glazebrook had argued. He accused these Oxbridge colleges of being willing to 'give a scholarship for classics to one who does not know what is the capital of Austria or the square of $a + x$; a scholarship for science to one who cannot construe Caesar or even spell common English words.' Yet he admitted that the schools were helpless until the universities themselves changed.

Now Oxford and Cambridge suddenly decided to offer places on A-levels or on conditional A levels. That, said Maland, was his lever with his senior colleagues to delay A levels in the school as long as possible. 'I exploited the Oxford and Cambridge changes which encouraged everyone to take A levels as late as possible,' he later confessed. So David Maland broadened the curriculum at Manchester, especially in the middle school. He deplored the tendency to rush boys through their courses, leaving them little time to reflect on what they were learning or realise that the subjects they were studying involved no easy solutions or obvious decisions. Early specialisation came to an end. Even the style of the boys' reports changed, giving much more space to general comments on a pupil's place in the school.

David Maland acknowledged and consolidated his predecessor's achievements by becoming chairman of the Headmasters' Conference Assisted Places Sub-Committee, by exploiting a Greater Manchester Council fund which was available to see a child through the first seven years of secondary education and by continuing to build up a school bursary fund with the help of generous old boys. The hostility of politically motivated local authorities was ceasing to matter, even though such decisions as that of Manchester City Council to prevent the mayor from taking up his *ex-officio* seat on the governing body still made headlines.

A new science block was built, flatteringly named after the historian who was High Master. Maland was pleased at its elegance for he deplored the physical appearance of the school. In the drab main corridor boys left their belongings in what were justly dubbed, cages. The Paton memorial library seemed to the High Master a neglected junk heap, 'a disaster area' in his own words. Maland swept away the cages; for two years a member of staff was seconded to the Paton library as librarian, and then a full-time librarian was

123

appointed; the library was sumptuously carpeted; thousands of pounds were spent on new books; and the boys' appetite for reading was further whetted by the installation of what must be the largest paperback bookshop in any school in Britain.

The High Master did his utmost to keep the school part of the independent educational community of Manchester and its conurbation. Not far away was a university hall of residence, Ashburne Hall. Here weekend conferences were arranged for teachers to confer together about their common problems, to offer each other their differing expertises and to make friends with each other. Every Saturday evening a bar at these conferences opened at 10.00 p.m. and did not close till early the following morning, while teachers hammered out points and questions.

'If your child passes our exams,' David Maland would tell parents, 'we have the right people here to help him develop those skills he has already displayed.' To cope with primary schools which were hostile to coaching for an eleven-plus or thirteen-plus exam, the Grammar School instituted a double entrance exam, one to discover a boy's competence in the straightforward skills, and a second to probe deeper. Again and again parents would tell David Maland that they were sending their boy to his school to get him into Oxford. Invariably the High Master would reply, 'Statistically, 40 per cent may go to Oxford or Cambridge, but there's no guarantee that your boy will be one of those.'

In 1983, after five years at Manchester, David Maland decided he wanted to give up his post. Traditionally High Masters of the Manchester Grammar School resigned only for some major new post – for example to found a new university. David Maland left to fulfil a long-held, long-frustrated ambition.

At Wadham College, Oxford, he had wanted to become a barrister. Instead he left to do national service and forgot about the law. The ambition faded away and David Maland became an historian and schoolmaster. In 1981 his son Oliver was called to the bar and his father's old ambition burst into flames again. As David Maland puts it, 'I was green with envy.' The High Master called on Raymond Baldwin to tell him he would resign in two years' time. Baldwin, supposing perhaps that David Maland was suffering from end-of-term fatigue, gave the High Master tea in his garden and a couple of plants. Six months passed and David Maland returned to confirm that he still planned to give up teaching. In consequence his successor, Geoffrey Parker, was appointed eighteen months before Maland left.

An historian, a Cambridge man, as tall a High Master as Eric James and Peter Mason, Geoffrey Parker came to Manchester at a time when feelings in the educational world were running high. Happily he had shared the problems of Peter Mason and David Maland as head of Wakefield Grammar School, fighting to raise bursaries as the direct grant system was destroyed and cheering up buildings that had deteriorated alarmingly for lack of cash.

He had also, in his National Service days, become a captain in the Royal Artillery, wryly commenting that at twenty-two he then possessed more

*Facing the future, Geoffrey Parker, High Master since 1985.*

authority than at any time until he became a head master. But at Manchester authority now needed tempering with diplomacy. The Government of the day had removed the right of state school teachers to negotiate over salaries and instead imposed wage 'settlements'. The independent schools were left with no bench marks against which to align there own wages structure. Industrial action was affecting state schools, and even at the Manchester Grammar School the common room salaries committee became uncharacteristically militant. In spite of harmonious agreements, life did not become easier. The school was obliged to rely on a continuous dialogue between the staff and the governors, with the High Master and Receiver in between.

Geoffrey Parker and his senior colleagues made several axiomatic assumptions. Whether state schools improved or declined in quality, the Manchester Grammar School would remain an academically selective school seeking pre-eminence in every field it entered. Its fees would be graded to ensure both that pupils could continue to be drawn from the widest possible social range and that masters (and now mistresses too) would be paid well enough to recruit the finest from among an increasingly limited supply of graduates. The team of senior masters also appraised the school accommodation: the needs of CDT and art, the demands of speech and drama, the expansion of physical geography.

They were also sensitive to the transformed relationship between the state and the independent sector in education. Neither of the two main political parties seemed likely to infuse the private sector with any more money. With a change in government the assisted places scheme might even be abolished. 'We are looking more and more to our own resources,' said Geoffrey Parker. Yet at the same time the Government appeared increasingly ready to coerce schools to accept its own ideals. The financial partnership with the state was still intact in the late 1980s, but the conditions under which it operated were changing.

Nonetheless an educational debate had opened up. A nationwide curriculum was about to be imposed. The training of young people from the ages of sixteen to nineteen was clearly a matter of deep concern. Fewer and fewer graduates were available as teachers. More positively, the independent schools no longer felt themselves threatened by the state. 'The defensive posture of the 1960s and 1970s is changing into a much more open position, because of the part we feel we ought to play in the national deliberations about these important educational issues,' said Geoffrey Parker. Thus his school braced itself for the 1990s.

In all this, had the Manchester Grammar School long forgotten its founder's aims? Certainly in two ways it had not. Hugh Oldham wanted children to be brought up in 'good learning and manners' and 'so that they might the better 'know, love, honour and dread God and his laws.' Godliness remains part of the school's tradition, though over the centuries its understanding of Godliness has widened. F. W. Walker told Lord Taunton that in matters of religion the school taught the boys the Church catechism and other portions of the Anglican Book of Common Prayer, but 'any boy whose parents object is

*In 1989 the cricket captains of the universities of Oxford and Cambridge were both Old Mancunians, Mark Crawley (right) and Michael Atherton. It was the first time for 84 years that the teams were captained by undergraduates from the same school.*

125

*Morning Assembly in the Memorial Hall.*

exempt,' he added. 'We have had Jews and Roman Catholics in the school.' By Paton's time the school included around 150 Jewish boys, so that at 9.05 each morning three fifteen minute assemblies took place, the upper school boys meeting in the art hall, the juniors in the main lecture theatre and the Jews in the chemistry lecture theatre. Eric James was proud that some 10 per cent of his schoolboys were Jewish (and equally proud that he took in the son of the secretary of the Arab League). School assemblies now take into account the fact that belief is not exclusively Christian.

Hugh Oldham was also concerned to educate boys of pregnant wit, regardless of the poverty or wealth of their parents. As Geoffrey Parker today puts it, 'We would still like to be able to admit young men of promise without regard to their parents' means.' The days of 2,000 entrance applicants were over. Now each year some 210 boys are being selected from around 500 would-be pupils. Yet the calibre of boys applying has not fallen. 'We have one great advantage,' declares the High Master. 'We are very famous in this locality.' In consequence the school still draws highly intelligent boys from an extraordinarily wide area and a remarkably broad social base.

The school strives to bring boys to what the founder called virtue, cunning and erudition. No narrow specialisation can produce such values, and the Manchester Grammar School has learned to eschew undue specialisation. This achievement took some time. 'Education,' J. L. Paton had preached, 'is not putting a boy in a groove and keeping him in it; it is getting him out of his groove and letting him see something of the largeness and infinite variety of life.' Narrow specialisation was thus to be abhorred. He believed that in the Manchester Grammar School and indeed in most English schools the classics and modern side had come to a *modus vivendi*. 'There has been give and take on both sides. The realists learn something of the humanities, the humanists learn something about the role of Nature.' Surprisingly enough this involved for him the teaching of his own pet subject, Latin. 'Latin is one of the connecting links between the Classical and the Modern side,' he held, useful not only to clergymen, doctors, apothecaries, historians, archaeologists and schoolmasters but also to the commercial man, for with Latin he would readily master French, Italian, Portuguese, Spanish and indeed any modern romance language in a quarter of the time normally taken, and he would also speak it better.

Holding such views Paton, making a rare appearance in Manchester in 1941 to lecture on the tercentenary of Comenius's visit to England, asked benignly, 'Do they not ask in the Clubs even to-day: "Where in all the world are we going to get our kitchen maids with all this education?"' He answered, 'Comenius's *Didactic* insists on the universality of education. The school is a place where all children are to be taught all subjects (*ubi omnes omnia omnino doceantur*).' One way Lord James had tried to ameliorate the specialisation of his school's curriculum was by fighting – in the teeth of opposition from several universities – for the new general paper at A level.

The Manchester Grammar School has remained aware of the dangers of over-specialisation. Today every boy spends five years in the school before choosing his A levels. Even then he is offered a dazzling range of additional options, none of which is examined. Chamber music, Chinese, short-stories, the world of Charles Dickens, the philosophy of Karl Marx, word processing, elementary karate, journalism, ceramics, the history of English architecture, and applied engineering, are merely a few of the general studies courses offered to sixth formers.

These courses are taught by staff who are in truth specialists in other subjects. But then, a powerfully motivated staff has long been the backbone of the Manchester Grammar School. As the High Master describes the school, it remains 'a very, very busy, even frantic place.' Being High Master of such a school is, he observed, 'like driving a coach pulled by thoroughbred racehorses.'

# Selected List of Old Mancunians

JOHN BRADFORD, 1510–1555. Protestant reformer and martyr.

LAURENCE VAUX, 1519–1585. Catholic divine and recusant.

JOHN BOOKER, 1603–1667. Astrologer and author in 1631 of *Telescopium Uranium*.

SAMUEL BOLTON, 1606–1654. Friend of Milton and University Preacher at Cambridge, he became rector of St Mark's, Ludgate.

JOHN WORTHINGTON, 1618–1671. Cambridge Platonist, fellow of Emmanuel College, and master of Jesus College from 1650.

NICHOLAS MOSLEY, 1611–1677. Entered Magdalene College, Cambridge, and wrote a Neoplatonic defence of Christianity entitled *The Soul of Man*. He fought as a Royalist and was knighted.

JOHN WOODWARD, 1665–1728. Professor of Geology at Gresham's College, London.

JAMES HEYWOOD, 1687–1776. A London linen-draper and journalist who became a Whig Alderman of the city. He told a fellow Mancunian 'not to make his son a dull plodding curate, but to send him to the city, and put him in the way of becoming a Sheriff or an Alderman of London.'

JOHN SHAW, 1713–1796. Manchester innkeeper noted for resolutely closing his inn every evening at 8 p.m. When Colonel Stanley was elected M.P. for the county, he took some friends to treat them at John Shaw's and asked to stay on after eight o'clock. Shaw replied, 'Colonel Stanley, you are a law-maker, and should not be a law-breaker; if you and your friends do not leave the room in five minutes, you will find your shoes full of water.'

JAMES BRADSHAW, 1720–46. Fought for Prince Charles Edward as a Trooper in Lord Elcho's Guards at Culloden, captured, tried in London, executed at Kennington 1746.

JOSEPH YATES, 1722–1770. Judge of the King's Bench in 1763, knighted, and transferred to the Common Pleas in the year of his death. Described by the *Gentleman's Magazine* as 'one of the honestest judges that ever lived.'

JOHN WATSON, 1724–1759. Antiquary, commoner of Brasenose, Anglican clergyman and author of a once celebrated *History of Halifax*.

THOMAS COPPOCK, 1730–1746. An exhibitioner of Brasenose College, he became a Jacobite and joined Prince Charles Stuart's insurrection in 1745. The following year he was executed.

JOHN WHITTAKER, 1735–1808. Historian, fellow of Corpus Christi College, Oxford, friend of Dr Johnson and enemy of Gibbon, to whom he wrote, 'You seem to me like another Tacitus, revived with all his animosity against Christianity.'

JOAB BATES, 1741–1799. Musician, conducted the music at Westminster Abbey in 1785 to commemorate the centenary of the birth of Handel.

JOHN CREWE, 1742–1828. High Sheriff of Cheshire, a Whig M.P., friend of Pitt, Greville and Fox and from 1806 Baron Crewe of Crewe.

PEPPER ARDEN, 1745–1804. Successively Attorney General, Solicitor General, Master of the Rolls and Lord Chief Justice of the Common Pleas, assumed the title of Lord Alvanley.

THOMAS JOHNSON, 1745–1823. Raised a regiment to fight in the American war of independence in 1770.

WILLIAM ARNALD, 1745–1802. Divine and commentator on holy scripture. He died insane.

THOMAS BRAITHWAITE, 1744–1800. Fellow of Brasenose College, and successively Archdeacon of Richmond and Archdeacon of Chester.

CYRIL JACKSON, 1743–1819. Dean of Christ Church, Oxford, who declined the Archbishopric of Canterbury.

WILLIAM JACKSON, 1751–1815. Canon of Christ Church, Oxford, Regius Professor of Greek and Bishop of Oxford from 1811.

GEORGE TRAVIS, 1741–1797. At St John's College, Cambridge, he was fifth senior *optime* and chancellor's medallist. As Archdeacon of Chester he attempted, unsuccessfully to defend against the onslaughts of Gibbon the spurious 1 John, chapter 5, verse 7, in the Authorized Version of the Bible.

THOMAS EGERTON, 1749–1814. Knight, Viscount and Earl.

PETER WRIGHT, 1759–1839. Fellow of Balliol and author of a poem in 1777 on the rebuilding of the Manchester Grammar School which includes the lines:
> Ah! heav'n born nymphs, so may ye not despise
> These lowly dwellings, where with holy awe
> The trembling youth his holy homage pays
> At learning's sacred shrine.

JOHN HOUGHTON, 1761–1787. Charles Lawson's favourite pupil, who had 'the glorious fever of talent' according to the High Master, and responded by writing of 'old Lawson's carking ways', describing him as 'Millgate's flogging Turk.'

ROBERT HOLT LEIGH, 1762–1843. Bart, MP for Wigan, went to Christ Church Oxford, but did not take his degree until he was 70. Reputed to be the greatest snuff-taker in England, rebuilt Hindley

Hall to his designs and forgot to put in a staircase.

JOSEPH ALLEN, 1770–1845. Bishop of Bristol, 1834, Bishop of Ely , 1836.

FRODSHAM HODSON, 1770–1822. Principal of Brasenose, Regious Professor of Divinity at Oxford, 1820.

JOHN TALBOT OF MALAHIDE, 1770–1851. Entered the Navy, served with Nelson, became an Admiral; appointed K.C.B.

JOHN WILLIAMS, 1777–1846. Attorney General, sentenced the Tolpuddle Martyrs in 1834 to penal servitude in Australia.

SAMUEL BAILEY, 1778–1864, Naval surgeon who served Nelson at Trafalgar.

ASSHURST TURNER GILBERT, 1786–1870. Principal of Brasenose College, 1822; Bishop of Chichester, 1842.

THOMAS H. MADDOCK, 1792–1870. Indian Civil Service, became Deputy Governor of Bengal, President of the Council of India; K.C.M.G.

THOMAS DE QUINCEY, 1785–1859. Author and opium-eater.

WILLIAM HIGGIN, 1794–1867. Bishop of Limerick, 1849; Bishop of Derry, 1853.

WILLIAM HARRISON AINSWORTH, 1805–1882. Extremely popular historical novelist and poet whose works include *Rookwood* and *The Lancashire Witches*. On leaving the school he wrote of his Alma Mater:

> For me, where'er my steps may go,
> Whate'er my future fate may be,

The current of my thoughts shall flow
With undiminished warmth to thee.

FREDERICK LINGARD, 1811–1847. Composer of sacred music.

HENRY GOUGH, 1812–1862. Headmaster of Carlisle Cathedral School.

ROBERT SCARR SOWLER, 1815–1871. Journalist and chief editorial writer on the *Manchester Courier* (which his father had founded). Barrister and one of the counsels for the prosecution at the Fenian trials of 1867.

WILLIAM ANDERTON SMITH, 1816–1870. Son of the High Master, he was ordained, and as a fervent high churchman and minor poet eventually became chaplain to the mineral water hospital, Bath. His verses include the lines:

> We love the Church, the House of God;
> We tred the path our fathers trod;
> And never will be Papists.

RICHARD CHAMBERS EDLESTON, 1816–1871. Cattle-breeder and agricultural innovator.

WILLIAM MACLURE, 1835–1901. Bart, M.P., Philanthropist.

JOSEPH WOOD, 1842–1921. Anglican clergyman and Headmaster of Harrow School.

FRANK LOCKWOOD, 1846–1897. Solicitor General, prosecuted Charles Peace, Skerry off the south coast of the Isle of Mull named after him: 'Frank Lockwood's Island'.

JOHN W. DIGGLE, 1847–1920. Bishop of Carlisle.

WILLIAM H. HEARD, 1847–1921. Headmaster of Fettes College, Edinburgh.

WILLIAM HOLLAND, 1849–1927. M.P., Cotton magnate, assumed the title of Lord Rotherham of Broughton.

WILLIAM GARRETT, 1852–1902. Took Holy Orders; in 1879 invented the first submarine, the *Resurgam* lost off the coast of North Wales, 1880.

LAZARUS FLETCHER, 1854–1921. F.R.S., Minerologist; appointed KB.

A. ATHERLEY-JONES, 1855–1921. K.C., Circuit Judge.

JOHN A. HAMILTON, 1859–1934. Lord Justice of Appeal; assumed the title of Viscount Sumner of Ibstone.

ERNEST BRAMAH SMITH, 1860–1942. 'Ernest Bramah', author of the Kai Lung series.

JOHN M. ASTBURY, 1860–1939. Judge of the High Court; appointed K.B.

JOHN C. WRIGHT, 1861–1933. Archbishop of Sydney and Primate of Australia.

HENRY BRERETON BAKER, 1862–1935. F.R.S., Prof. of Chemistry, Imperial College of Science.

FREDERICK S. KIPPING, 1863–1949. F.R.S., Prof. of Chemistry, Nottingham University.

ARTHUR J. POLLOCK, 1863–1922. F.R.S., third Prof. of Physics, Sydney University, Australia.

DANIEL HALL, 1864–1942. F.R.S., Head of Rothamstead; member of the Development Commission, appointed K.B.

ARTHUR DENDY, 1865–1925. F.R.S., Prof. of Zoology, London University.

GERALD SHARP, 1865–1933. Archbishop of Brisbane.

DAVID L. CHAPMAN, 1869–1958. F.R.S., Tutor, Jesus College, Oxford.

FRANK W. GAMBLE, 1869–1925. F.R.S., Prof. of Zoology, Birmingham University.

GORDON HEWART, 1870–1943. Solicitor General, Attorney General then, from 1922–40, Lord Chief Justice of England;

assumed the title of Viscount Hewart of Bury.

JOHN S. BRADBURY, 1873–1950. Permanent Secretary to the Treasury. £1 and 10s notes with his signature were known as 'Bradbury' notes; assumed the title of Lord Bradbury Winsford.

EDMUND T. WHITTAKER, 1873–1956. F.R.S., Astronomer Royal for Ireland at the age of 31; Prof. of Mathematics, Edinburgh University; appointed K.B.

JAMES EVERSHED AGATE, 1874–1947. Author and critic.

ERNEST BARKER, 1874–1960. Political scientist and fellow of Peterhouse, Cambridge, 1928–1939; knighted 1944.

THOMAS A. CHAPMAN, 1876–1949. Bishop of Colchester.

BERNARD SPILSBURY, 1877–1947. Forensic Medical Expert; appointed K.B.

SIDNEY ARNOLD, 1878–1945. Postmaster General 1929–31; assumed the title of Lord Arnold of Hale.

THOMAS C. DUGDALE, 1880–1952. Artist; A.R.A. 1936; R.A. 1943.

EDWIN T. ENGLAND, 1880–1945. Chief Master, King Edward VI School, Birmingham.

RICHARD G. PARSONS, 1881–1976. Bishop of Southwark, Bishop of Hereford.

WILLIAM STANLEY HOUGHTON, 1881–1913. Unpaid drama critic of the *Manchester City News*, 1905–1913, and dramatist (*Hindle Wakes*).

HARRY BATEMAN, 1882–1946. F.R.S., Prof. of Maths and Theoretical Physics, California Institute of Technology.

HAROLD BRIGHOUSE, 1882–1958. Playwright and novelist.

KENNETH FISHER, 1882–1945. Headmaster of Oundle School.

BEN IDEN PAYNE, 1882–1976. Actor and theatre manager, with Sir Frank Benson and Miss Horniman; produced in 1915, for the first time anywhere, Harold Brighouse's *Hobson's Choice* in New York; Prof. Emeritus of Drama, University of Texas.

HENRY LAMB, 1883–1960. War artist. R.A. 1949.

FREDERICK JAMES MARQUIS, 1883–1964. Businessman and Conservative politician; knighted 1935 and created 1st Earl of Woolton 1955.

NORMAN P. H. WHITLEY, 1883–1957. Chief Justice of Uganda; appointed K.B.

CHARLES C. GIBSON, 1884–1950. F.R.S., Prof. of Chemistry, Guy's Hospital Medical School.

JOHN LEIGH, 1884–1959. M.P., Philanthropist, gave a park to Altrincham; created Baronet.

JOHN SIMONSEN, 1884–1956. F.R.S., Prof. of Chemistry, various Universities, appointed K.B.

DAVID M. S. WATSON, 1886–1973, F.R.S., Geologist.

GEOFFREY JEFFERSON, 1886–1961. F.R.S., Neurologist; appointed K.B.

SIMON MARKS, 1888–1964. In 1916 became chairman of Marks and Spencer, the company founded by his father Michael in 1884. Together with his former school-fellow and brother-in-law Israel Sieff (they each married the other's sister) built up the company to its internationally famous status. Both men were convinced Zionists. Marks was knighted in 1944 and made a baron in 1961.

JOHN S. B. STOPFORD, 1888–1961. F.R.S., Vice-Chancellor of Manchester University, Prof. of Anatomy; assumed the title of Lord Stopford of Fallowfield.

ISRAEL MOSES SIEFF, 1889–1972. Married the sister of his school friend Simon Marks and became vice-chairman of Marks and Spencer in 1926, succeeding Simon Marks as chairman in 1964. A philanthropist and a Zionist, he became a personal assistant to Chaim Weizmann, as well as a chairman of the discussion group Political and Economic Planning. A fellow of the Royal Anthropological Society, he was created a life peer in 1966.

LAWRENCE DU GARDE PEACH, 1890–1974. Dramatist

GEORGE NORMAN CLARK, 1890–1979. Historian. Oxford Brackenbury scholar, 1908, prize fellow of All Souls 1912. A prisoner of war between 1916 and 1918, he returned to take up a fellowhip at Oriel in 1919. He was successively Chichele professor of economic history, 1931; Regius Professor of Modern History at Cambridge, 1943, and a fellow of Trinity. Made Provost of Oriel 1947, he was knighted in 1953.

BEN POLLARD, 1890–1967. Bishop of Sodor and Man.

JAMES H. BARNES, 1891–1966. Permanent Under Secretary of State for Air; appointed K.C.B., K.B.E.

HENRY DAVENPORT KAY, 1893–1977. F.R.S., Chemist.

HAROLD LASKI, 1893–1950. Labour political theorist and Professor of Politics at the University of London.

WALTER C. HANKINSON, 1894–1973. U.K. Ambassador in Dublin; appointed K.C.M.G.

THOMAS H. ELLIS, 1894–1972. Chief Justice, High Court; Acting Governor of Bengal; appointed K.B.

LOUIS GOLDING, 1895–1958, Novelist, playwright and traveller.

HUGH EMLYN JONES, 1902– . Circuit Judge.

DOUGLAS G. A. LOWE, 1902–1981. Winner of the 800 metres in the Olympic Games in 1924 and 1928.

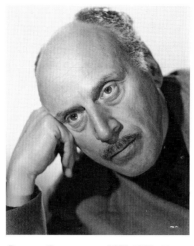

GEORGE COULOURIS, 1903–1989. Eccentric, actor, film star and a founder member of Orson Welles's Mercury players.

ALEXANDER OPPENHEIM, 1903– . Vice-Chancellor, University of Malaysia; appointed K.B.

JOHN PEEL, 1904– . Physician to H.M. The Queen; appointed K.C.V.O.

LESLIE MAURICE LEVER, 1905–1979. Philanthropist and Labour politician. Lord Mayor of Manchester, 1977–1978. Life peer 1975; Knight Grand Cross of the Order of St Gregory the Great, 1968.

JOHN EDWARD SIEFF, 1905–1982. Joined Marks & Spencer, successively Joint Managing Director, Chairman, President and Honorary President.

RICHARD WHITTINGTON, 1905–1975. H.M. Ambassador to Thailand; appointed K.C.M.G.

EDGAR LUSTGARTEN, 1907–1978. Author, journalist, broadcaster.

EDGAR A. COHEN, 1908–1973. British Representative, O.E.C.D.; appointed K.C.M.G.

PHILIP CURTIS, 1908– . Circuit Judge.

DONALD GIBSON, 1908– . Architect of post-war Coventry, knight.

CYRIL RAY, 1908– . Writer, wine-lover.

HORACE TAYLOR, 1908– . R.N.V.R.; awarded the George Cross 1941.

JAMES CARRERAS, 1909– . Chairman, Duke of Edinburgh's Award Scheme; appointed K.C.V.O.; K.B.

GEORGE H. ANDREW, 1910– . Permanent Secretary, Ministry of Education; appointed K.C.M.G.

JOHN S. BEAVAN, 1910– . Journalist; assumed the title of Lord Beavan of Ardwick.

JOSEPH CANTLEY, 1910–. High Court Judge, Queen's Bench Division, knight.

GORDON WHEELER, 1910–. The Rt Revd Monsignor, Bishop of Leeds.

GEOFFREY M. WILSON, 1910– . Chairman, Race Relations Board; appointed K.C.B.

MICHAEL SIEFF, 1911–1987. Joined Marks & Spencer, successively Director, Asst Managing Director, Chairman.

JOHN W. S. PRINGLE, 1912–1983. F.R.S., Zoologist.

JACK S. R. ABDELA, 1913– . Q.C., Judge, Central Criminal Court.

FRANK ALLAUN, 1913– . Journalist and Labour M.P.

MARCUS SIEFF, 1913–. Chairman (1972–1984) and now president of Marks and Spencer, was, with his father Israel, the first father and son to be individually created Life Peers. Amongst many business positions he holds, is the non-executive chairmanship of *The Independent* newspaper. He also holds honorary degrees from five universities.

HENRY N. BARBER, 1914–1971. F.R.S., Prof. of Botany, University of N.S.W., Australia.

HAROLD LEVER, 1914–. Politician; financial secretary to the treasury, 1967–1969 and life peer 1970.

ENRIQUE WILD, 1914– . Bishop of Reading.

DAVID J. FINNEY, 1917– . F.R.S., Statistician.

MARK B. SMITH, 1917– . Circuit Judge.

JAMES BADDILEY, 1918– . F.R.S., Prof. of Organic Chemistry, Newcastle University; appointed K.B.

MICHAEL PLATT WINSTANLEY, 1918– . Liberal M.P., broadcaster and life peer 1975.

HARRY HARRIS, 1919– . F.R.S., Prof. of Biochemistry, King's College, London.

LEO PLIATSKY, 1919– . Civil servant; knighted 1977.

QUINTON HAZELL, 1920– . Industrialist.

THOMAS H. PIGOT, 1921– . Common Sergeant, City of London; Master of the Bench, Inner Temple.

WIGODER, LORD, 1921– . Chief Whip of the Liberal Party in the House of Lords, 1977–1984.

FRANK COOPER, 1922– . Civil servant; P.C., G.C.B.

JOHN DICKINSON, 1922– . Industrialist; Founder of Flow Flex Group, Engineering.

WILLIAM H. W. JALLAND, 1922– . Circuit Judge.

GEORGE W. KENNER, 1922–1978. F.R.S., Prof. of Organic Chemistry, Liverpool University.

WILLIAM BARLOW, 1924– . Chairman of the Post Office, 1977–1980; chairman of B.I.C.C. and Knight.

ROBERT OXTON BOLT, 1924– . Playwright. C.B.E. 1972.

PETER W. GOLDSTONE, 1926– . Circuit Judge.

KENNETH C. TURPIN, 1926– . Provost of Oriel College, Oxford, Vice-Chancellor of Oxford University.

BENET ALAN HYTNER, 1927– . Crown Court Recorder, Judge of Appeal, Isle of Man.

JOHN C. M. MASON, 1927– . High Commissioner, Australia; appointed K.C.M.G.

DESMOND FRANKS, 1928– . Circuit Judge.

MICHAEL HENSHALL, 1928– . Bishop of Warrington.

GEOFFREY JOHNSON TORDOFF, 1928– . Chairman of the Liberal Party, 1976–1979, life peer, SLD Chief Whip, House of Lords, 1988.

MICHAEL FRANCIS ATIYA, 1929– . Mathematician, F.R.S., knighted 1983, appointed Master of Trinity College, Cambridge, 1990.

JOHN CHARLES POLANYI, 1929– . Professor of Physics, Toronto University, and Nobel Prize winner.

ROY COOKE, 1930– . Director, Coventry Schools.

DOUGLAS D. BROWN, 1931– . Judge of the High Court; appointed K.B.

DAVID S. GANDY, 1932– . Deputy Director and General Executive, Public Prosecutions, Crown Prosecution Services.

ALAN GARNER, 1934– . Teenage fiction writer.

JOHN OGDON, 1937–1989. Pianist and composer.

BEN KINGSLEY, 1943– . Actor and film star.

ROBERT POWELL, 1944– . Actor and film star.

MICHAEL D. WOOD, 1948– . TV Presenter, historical series.

STEPHEN C. PIMLOTT, 1953– . Opera Producer.

NICHOLAS ROBERT HYTNER, 1956–. Theatre director, opera producer, director of the Royal Exchange Theatre, Manchester.

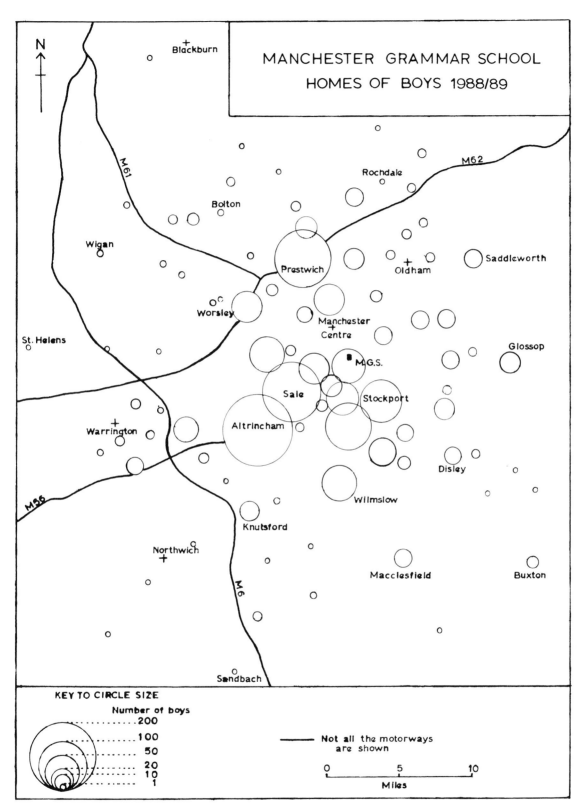

MANCHESTER GRAMMAR SCHOOL
HOMES OF BOYS 1988/89

KEY TO CIRCLE SIZE

Number of boys

200
100
50
20
10
1

Not all the motorways are shown

0    5    10
Miles

(An interesting comparison can be made with the 1895 map on p. 87.)

# INDEX

(The figures in italics refer to illustrations)